A Poetry Teacher's Toolkit

Book 3: Style, Shape and Structure

Other titles in this series:

A Poetry Teacher's Toolkit Book 1: Words and Wordplay
A Poetry Teacher's Toolkit Book 2: Rhymes, Rhythms and Rattles
A Poetry Teacher's Toolkit Book 4: Language and Performance

A Poetry Teacher's Toolkit

Book 3:
Style, Shape and Structure

Collette Drifte and Mike Jubb

David Fulton Publishers
London

David Fulton Publishers Ltd
Ormond House, 26–27 Boswell Street, London WC1N 3JZ
www.fultonpublishers.co.uk

First published in Great Britain in 2002 by David Fulton Publishers

Note: The rights of Collette Drifte and Mike Jubb to be identified as the authors of this work have been asserted by them in accordance with the Copyright, Designs and Patents Act 1988.

Copyright © 2002 Collette Drifte and Mike Jubb

British Library Cataloguing in Publication Data
A catalogue record for this book is available from the British Library.

ISBN 1-85346-820-7

Typeset by Kenneth Burnley, Wirral, Cheshire
Illustrations by Bethan Metthews
Printed and bound in Great Britain by Bell and Bain Ltd, Glasgow

Contents

For Reinhard [C.D.]

For Brian Moses, for his help and encouragement [M.J.]

The Authors

Collette Drifte is a former deputy head teacher who has 23 years' experience in both mainstream and special primary education. She has specialised in both learning difficulties and child language development and disorders, and spent nine years working as a special educational needs advisory teacher to mainstream practitioners. Now a freelance author, lecturer and in-service education and training (INSET) provider, her writing credits include: *Phonicability* (Hopscotch Educational Publishing 2000); *Including Lower-achievers in the Literacy Hour: Using Stories and Poems* (Hopscotch Educational Publishing 2001); *Foundations for the Literacy Hour* (Step Forward Publishing 2001); and *Special Needs in Early Years Settings* (David Fulton Publishers 2001). Other publications include articles in the *Times Educational Supplement* and *Practical Pre-School*, and regular articles and reviews for *Nursery World*.

Mike Jubb is a primary school teacher who lives in Hampshire with his two children, Nicky and Kevin. Having waited until middle age before discovering that he might be able to write, Mike has had many poems anthologised and his own collection, *Burblings of the Jubb-Jubb Bird*, is available for £4.50 (including post and packing) from Mike Jubb, PO Box 245, Fareham, Hants PO15 6YN.

Acknowledgements

We would like to thank the following, without whom these books would never have been written: Helen Fairlie, of David Fulton Publishers, for her untold patience in dealing with a never-ending stream of queries and for her valued suggestions; Alan Worth, also of David Fulton Publishers, for his efficient and professional friendliness in steering us through the production process; those friends and professionals who tried out the activities and made suggestions; staff and pupils of Rupert House School, Henley-on-Thames, Redlands Primary School, Fareham, Peel Common Junior School, Gosport and Crofton Hammond Junior School, Stubbington; and, finally, our families, for their support and tolerance, even when we were up the walls or in our rooms sulking.

Collette Drifte
Mike Jubb

The authors and the publishers would like to thank the following copyright holders for permission to include their work:

Elizabeth Bailey, for 'The Bewitching Hour'.

Gerard Benson, for 'Earth Apples', from *The Magnificent Callisto*, published by Blackie/ Puffin, 1992, and *To Catch an Elephant*, published by Smith-Doorstop, 2002, © Gerard Benson.

Nathan Bethell, for 'I love, I HATE'.

Paul Bright, for 'Call that Music?'

Amy Bulpitt, for 'My Mum'.

Sophie Calthorpe, for 'The Moon Poem'.

Jane Clarke, for 'Roasting the Phoenix'.

Gina Douthwaite, for 'Shadow', from *Picture a Poem*, published by Hutchinson, 1994, and 'Rhino', from *Whacky Wild Animals*, published by Macmillan, 2000, both poems © Gina Douthwaite.

Elizabeth Bailey, for 'The Bewitching Hour'.

Dan Fisher, for 'The Moon'.

Robert Fisher, for 'The Phoenix', from *Amazing Monsters*, published by Faber and Faber Ltd, 1982.

Philip Gross, for 'Daughter of the Sea', from *All-Nite Café*, published by Faber and Faber Ltd, reprinted by permission of Faber and Faber Ltd.

Brian Moses, for 'Dreamer', from *Hippopotamus Dancing*, published by Cambridge University Press, 1994, © Brian Moses.

Rachael Oliver, for 'Up in the Sky'.

Sheila Simmons, for 'In the Wood', from *Another First Poetry Book*, edited by John Foster and published by Oxford University Press, 1987, © Sheila Simmons.

Katy Ware, for 'The Moon'.

Celia Warren, for 'Today's the Day', from *Where Oak Birds Sing*, published by The Lichfield Press, © Celia Warren, 2000.

Every effort has been made to trace copyright holders, but in some instances this has not been possible. The publishers would like to apologise for any errors or omissions in this list, and would be grateful to be advised of any corrections which should be made to future editions of this book.

Introduction

The package deal

Even though my teaching days are over – they are now a source of anecdotes and amusing stories to weave into my lectures – I am aware that there are still unplugged holes that cause teachers to question 'Why doesn't somebody invent an xxx to do that?' or state 'Someone ought to write a book which covers that'. We aim to 'cover that' with this series of books, 'that' being poetry and the teaching thereof.

In my pre-National Curriculum days I taught a literature syllabus, both prose and poetry, which covered most, if not all (and more!), of the objectives in the National Literacy Strategy – nothing new there really. I can still remember spending lunchtimes and evenings searching through poetry anthologies for suitable poems to illustrate a specific teaching point – nothing new in that either. In fact, from comments made to me on my rounds since hanging up my satchel, this is still quite a problem. The 'big poetry hunt' eats into what precious little time teachers have left in their 24 hours after preparation, marking, form-filling, etc. I recall one child's face registering utter surprise as he realised I had a home to go to – 'Don't you sleep here, then, Miss?' he asked. Sometimes it felt as if I did!

We all know that there is a healthy supply of poetry anthologies available (many based on themes), which are beautifully produced, superbly illustrated and packed with, in some cases, hundreds of poems – but how does a teacher zoom straight to those that illustrate specific points such as alliteration, wordplay, metaphors and similes? This is where we come in. *A Poetry Teacher's Toolkit* is aimed at Key Stage 2 teachers who need to teach poetry as part of the National Literacy Strategy whether by choice, design or default. It brings together a collection of poems that offers quick access to such specific points, inspirational ideas and more formalised lesson plans, together with supporting photocopiable differentiated activity sheets. The book provides a complete package that should help teachers to maximise their limited preparation and research time.

The myth exploders

There is another, equally important, reason why this series of books was written. Poetry is often perceived as a medium that is 'difficult', 'highbrow', 'hard to teach' or 'not cool'. However you may feel about poetry, it is now a prominent part of the National Literacy Strategy.

In this series, we aim to demystify poetry in a fun way that will inspire enthusiasm in both you and the kids you teach. We offer ideas and suggestions that will both stimulate and excite anyone who happens to be in your room while you are 'doing' poetry. Reading and writing poetry is fun as well as educational, and we make no apologies for putting this message across with gusto! Activities are suggested that not only extend and consolidate the teaching points made in the lessons but also simultaneously – and almost unconsciously – foster an enjoyment of poetry by everyone.

The Toolkit

We are very aware that you, as teachers, are hard-pressed for time as well as bound by the requirements of the National Curriculum. *A Poetry Teacher's Toolkit* provides lesson plans that follow the framework of the Literacy Hour and support specific objectives in the National Literacy Strategy. The lesson plans are based on poems from the collection and include photocopiable activity sheets that support each teaching point and which are differentiated, thereby reducing preparation time. Many a teacher has told us that they would have our arms out of the sockets if we proffered such a book! It would be arrogant of us to suggest that these lesson plans are The Answer, but they offer a framework that you can either use as it stands, or tweak and cherry-pick to suit your own or your school's requirements. Because some of you may not normally 'teach' poetry, we have scripted the lessons. Before you gasp in outrage this is purely for guidance – the lessons can and should be delivered in your own personal style.

Chapter and verse

Each chapter follows the same format, which you will quickly become familiar with as you use the ideas and lessons:

- A list of featured poems and poets relevant to the chapter's contents.
- Ideas and suggestions for the reading, writing and performance of poetry by both children and teachers.
- More formalised lesson plans in line with the structure and recommendations of the Literacy Hour including relevant National Literacy Strategy objectives for Years 3–6 (at text, sentence and word level), materials needed, preparation required and scripted sessions.
- Photocopiable activity sheets differentiated for lower, average and higher achievers. Each sheet presents the same activity at appropriate levels and is differentiated as follows:
     sheets a or aa for the lower achievers
     sheets b or bb for the average achievers
     sheets c or cc for the higher achievers.
- The featured poems reproduced for reference.

We have offered the material in such a way that will allow you to use it at whatever level you want, whether as an activity done outside the Literacy Hour or as an integral part of the hour itself, and to whatever degree you want, such as incorporating several more of the activities into one of the lessons or taking a lesson plan as the basis for deeper exploration of the teaching point. Virtually all of the Literacy Hour lesson plans have at least one group activity suggestion from the previous part of the chapter, but you don't have to stick rigidly to that. You know your kids and the areas that need to be reinforced or consolidated. Use the Toolkit to pick and mix but, above all, have fun!

Style, Shape and Structure and the National Literacy Strategy – comfortable bedfellows

In this section we have isolated those points in the National Literacy Strategy that have a particular bearing on the topics covered by this volume. This will help you to focus your mind and write your lesson plans.

Year 3

Term 1

To read aloud and recite poems; to distinguish between rhyming and non-rhyming poetry; to express their views about a . . . poem, identifying specific words and phrases to support their viewpoint; to generate ideas relevant to a topic by brainstorming, word association, etc.; to collect suitable words and phrases, in order to write poems and short descriptions; design simple patterns with words, use repetitive phrases; to invent calligrams and a range of shape poems; to use awareness of grammar to decipher new or unfamiliar words; to take account of the grammar and punctuation . . . when reading aloud; to experiment with deleting words in sentences to see which are essential to retaining meaning and which are not; to use word banks and dictionaries; to infer the meaning of unknown words from the context; to understand the purpose and organisation of the thesaurus and to make use of it to find synonyms.

Term 2

To . . . prepare poems for performance, identifying appropriate expression, tone, volume and use of voices and other sounds; to rehearse and improve performance, taking note of punctuation and meaning; to write new or extended verses for performance based on models of 'performance' and oral poetry read; to experiment with deleting words in sentences to see which are essential to retain meaning and which are not; to use awareness of grammar to decipher new or unfamiliar words; to take account of the grammar and punctuation . . . when reading aloud; to use word banks and dictionaries; to infer the meaning of unknown words from the context; to continue the collection of new words from reading and . . . make use of them in reading and writing.

Term 3

To compare forms or types of humour by exploring . . . word play; to select, prepare, read aloud and recite by heart poetry that plays with language or entertains; to recognise rhyme, alliteration and other patterns of sound that create effects; to write poetry that uses sound to create effects, e.g. onomatopoeia . . . distinctive rhythms; to use awareness of grammar to decipher new or unfamiliar words; to take account of the grammar and punctuation . . . when reading aloud; to use word banks and dictionaries; to infer the meaning of unknown words from the context.

Year 4

Term 1

To find out more about popular authors, poets and discuss personal responses and preferences; to write poems based on personal or imagined experience, linked to poems read; to list brief phrases and words; to reread own writing to check for grammatical sense and accuracy; to revise work on verbs . . . and to investigate verb tenses; to use phonic/spelling knowledge as a cue, together with graphic, grammatical and contextual knowledge, when reading unfamiliar texts; to define familiar vocabulary in their own words.

Term 2

To identify different patterns of rhyme and verse in poetry; to write poetry based on the structure and/or style of poems read; to understand the significance of word order; to use alternative words or expressions which are more accurate and interesting than common choices.

Term 3

To describe how a poet does or does not use rhyme; to recognise some simple forms of poetry; to read further . . . poems by a favourite writer, making comparisons and identifying familiar features of the writer's work; to write poems, experimenting with different styles and structures, discuss if and why different forms are more suitable than others; to produce polished poetry through revision; to identify the common punctuation marks . . . and respond to them appropriately when reading; to use phonic/spelling knowledge as a cue, together with graphic, grammatical and contextual knowledge, when reading unfamiliar texts.

Year 5

Term 1

To analyse and compare poetic style, use of forms and themes of significant poets; to explain and justify personal tastes (in poetry); to understand the basic conventions of standard English; to discuss, proofread and edit their own writing for clarity and correctness; to use dictionaries and IT spell checks.

Term 2

To perform poems in a variety of ways; to use the structures of poems read to write extensions based on these; to understand how writing can be adapted for different . . . purposes; to consolidate the conventions of standard English; to use dictionaries and IT spell checks; to investigate metaphorical expressions.

Term 3

To read, rehearse and modify performance of poetry; to use performance poems as models to write and produce poetry in polished forms through revising, redrafting and presentation; to secure the basic conventions of standard English; to understand how writing can be adapted for different audiences; to use a range of dictionaries and understand their purposes.

Year 6

Term 1

To articulate personal responses to literature, identifying why and how a text affects the reader; to contribute constructively to shared discussion about literature, responding to and building on the views of others; produce revised poems for reading aloud individually; to revise the conventions of standard English; to use dictionaries.

Term 2

To recognise how poets manipulate words; to analyse how messages, moods, feelings and attitudes are conveyed in poetry; to read and interpret poems in which meanings are implied or multi-layered; to discuss, interpret challenging poems with others; to increase familiarity with significant poets and writers of the past; to continue work on grammatical awareness and sentence construction and punctuation; to use dictionaries and IT spell checks.

Term 3

To describe and evaluate the style of an individual poet; to comment critically on the overall impact of a poem; to write a sequence of poems linked by theme or form; to continue work on grammatical awareness and sentence construction and punctuation; to experiment with language, e.g. creating . . . similes and metaphors.

Right, on with the motley – or at least the sessions, whether you wear funny togs or not! The main thing to remember is that you should all be having fun during these sessions, so throw caution and dignity to the wind, get yourself to the level of the kids and enjoy yourselves.

A 'Must Read' Chapter!

Read this chapter if you read none of the others!

'I get a fine warm feeling when I'm doing well, but that pleasure is pretty much negated by the pain of getting started each day. Let's face it, writing is hell.' (William Styron)

That just about sums up the love/hate affair that many professional writers have with their craft. But they are volunteers, and deserve no sympathy whatsoever.

The ones we **should** feel sorry for are the press-ganged kids who are obliged to 'write a story' or 'write a poem', whether they feel inspired or not (usually not!). For many of them, it really **must** be hell, and it can be pretty hellish for the teacher trying to inspire them too!

This is a 'bullet-point' chapter, designed to help you all towards poetry heaven.

Your attitude

- If you're uncertain about teaching poetry, you're reading the right book.
- If you're not yet enthusiastic about poetry, FAKE IT for now because you soon will be! As in everything else, enthusiasm from the teacher equals enthusiasm from the kids.
- You won't overcome barriers in the mind of a child until you overcome any that **you** might have in yours.
- Nobody likes **all** poetry, so give yourself a chance and find out what you **do** like. Children's poetry is an easy read – soak yourself in it.
- Start a loose-leaf collection of your favourites, and make your own booklist. Leave it lying around for the kids to browse through and let them see you browsing through it.
- Please don't think of poetry as a 'subject' to be covered. If you want success, it should be ever-present.
- Algebra is for schooldays. Poetry is for life.
- Petition for an INSET day with an established children's poet.
- Arrange for a performance poet to come into school.
- It's good to ring the changes – try a different poet each term.

Creating a poetry atmosphere

- Have a good, and constantly changing, selection of poetry books and tapes in your classroom, and allow time for the children to explore them.
- Make your own poetry tapes, and encourage the children and tame parents to do the same.
- Read a new poem to your class each day, maybe in the ten minutes before lunch (see 'Appreciation and analysis' for a suggested strategy).
- Sometimes read narrative poetry at 'story time'.
- Get the children to write out, **at home**, the words of their favourite pop songs and adverts, and bring the transcripts in.
- Please don't just have a poetry 'unit' and think 'Well, I've done poetry now'. 'A little and often' will show that you really value poetry. You can slip a poem in almost anywhere by linking it with other themes, such as the weather or festivals. And if you can't find a poem to fit, write one yourself. Yes you can!
- Display a 'Poem of the Week'. Choose a reasonably short one so that each child can copy it into a special book, along with their own favourites, to create a personal anthology. This is copying with a purpose – it's allowed.
- Use poetry for handwriting practice.
- Use all your display skills to show off children's own poetry in exciting ways; 'publication' of their work is vital.
- Encourage and reward learning poetry by heart. It's fun.
- Encourage performance of poems learnt. The sense of achievement is huge.
- Would you, or one of your colleagues, be willing to start a school 'Poetry Choir'? (See *A Poetry Teacher's Toolkit* Book 4, Ch. 4.)
- Create illustrated class anthologies either by theme, or with each child choosing a favourite.
- **Every classroom should have a flipchart**. When you're writing a poem with the whole class, or brainstorming, or making word collections, or experimenting with any kind of wordplay, it's worth keeping the results as a possible future resource.
- TOP TIP for encouraging children to write poetry: write poetry yourself. Yes you **can**!

On being a writer

- Teachers often say that they can't write poetry – but they ask children to!
- Poetry has something special going for it. Not everyone can write a novel, but **everyone** can write poetry.
- If, for argument's sake, Shakespeare lives at the top of the poetry skyscraper, and nursery rhymes dwell on the ground floor, it follows that there is a room for everyone.
- Everyone **can** write poetry and every primary school teacher **should** write poetry.
- 'The worst thing you write is better than the best thing you didn't write' (Unknown).
- 'If you would be a writer, first be a reader' (Allan W. Eckert).
- Children learn to speak through imitation, not by constantly being corrected. Is there a lesson for writing here?

- 'Read everything . . . trash, classics, good and bad, and see how they do it. Read! You'll absorb it. Then write' (William Faulkner).
- Some people think that it's unreasonable to expect the whole class to write about the same thing at the same time. Well, many of the poems that **I** write come about because an anthologist has requested poems about a particular subject. This 'restriction' frees my mind of other topics and tells me what to concentrate on. If all the children are writing about the same thing, ideas start buzzing around. We don't want outright copying, but writers are always pinching (sorry, 'adapting') each other's ideas.
- 'Writing is a form of therapy; sometimes I wonder how all those who do not write, compose or paint can manage to escape the madness, melancholia, the panic fear which is inherent in a human situation' (Graham Greene).

Inspiration

Hopefully, you will find much in this series to inspire both you and your children, but here are a few quotations on the subject:

- 'I write when I'm inspired, and I see to it that I'm inspired at nine o'clock every morning' (Peter De Vries). In other words, you have to **make** it happen.
- 'The art of writing is the art of applying the seat of the pants to the seat of the chair' (Mary Heaton Vorse).
- 'The ideal view for daily writing, hour on hour, is the blank brick wall of a cold storage warehouse' (Edna Ferba).
- 'Imagination is more important than knowledge' (Einstein).

Drafting and redrafting

- 'The beautiful part of writing is that you don't have to get it right the first time, unlike, say, a brain surgeon' (Robert Cormier).
- 'It is perfectly okay to write garbage – as long as you edit brilliantly' (C. J. Cherryh).
- 'There is no great writing, only great rewriting' (Justice Brandeis).
- 'I have made this letter longer than usual, only because I have not had the time to make it shorter' (Blaise Pascal).
- 'In composing, as a general rule, run your pen through every other word you have written; you have no idea what vigour it will give to your style' (Sydney Smith).
- Successful creative writing is not about individual lessons, it's about creating an atmosphere in which children feel free to take risks. And if you weren't already convinced about the importance of rewriting, I hope you are now. Your mission, should you choose to accept it, is to persuade the children!
- Children should feel liberated by the thought that professional writers don't get it right first time; that they don't begin at the beginning, go through the middle, get to the end . . . and that's it.
- The beginning/middle/end thing is an important concept, for the reader or listener; but the **writer** doesn't have to work that way, providing the outcome has structure.

- We need to relax children about creative writing. We must persuade them that they can't get it 'wrong' in a first draft. Of course, we can help them to improve their writing but, if we're too judgemental, we'll scare them off.
- For the first draft: **no rubbers and no spellings**. They slow down creativity. The most important thing is to get words onto paper as quickly as possible. Errors can be put right and improvements made – later. It's counter-productive to ask children to be creative, and then burden them (or allow them to burden themselves) with secretarial matters that could be sorted out after the poem or story has evolved.
- 'Show, don't tell', e.g. 'She was angry' merely TELLS us about her anger; but 'She threw her hairbrush at the mirror' SHOWS us her anger. It's far more powerful writing. (See *A Poetry Teacher's Toolkit* Book 4, Ch. 1.)
- When writing, we tend to concentrate on the visual to the neglect of our other senses. That's a waste of resources. (Again, see *A Poetry Teacher's Toolkit* Book 4, Ch. 1.)
- Always be SPECIFIC. Don't say 'I saw a dog', say 'I saw a white poodle'. There are many opportunities to improve writing by this simple trick of the trade. (For more information about being specific, see *A Poetry Teacher's Toolkit* Book 4.)
- The second draft is not just a neater copy of the first.
- All words are not born equal. If you can cut out a word, and the poem doesn't 'miss' it, then cut it out (the same applies to prose).
- The poem's title is always the last thing that I write so that it fits what I have written and not the other way round.
- 'Don't be afraid to be bad. Every drop of high-performance gasoline starts as crude oil' (R. E. Lee).

Grammar

- Grammar to a poet is almost a total irrelevance.
- By 1870, there were no professors of modern English at Oxford and Cambridge.
- Grammar is based on Latin and ancient Greek . . . wonderful languages for grammarians because they are DEAD, and the rules can be fossilised. That's why we have such weary commandments as: never begin a sentence with 'And' or 'But'; never split an infinitive; never end a sentence with prepositions such as 'with', 'on', 'to', 'for'.
- 'In the beginning, God created the heaven and the earth. And the earth was without form and void; and darkness was on the face of the deep. And the spirit of God moved upon the face of the waters. And God said, "Let there be light": and there was light. And God called the light day, and the darkness he called night. And the evening and the morning were the first day.' Five sentences beginning with 'And'.

Grammar has its place, but it shouldn't get in the way of what we want to say, or the way we want to say it.

Ne'er more these things a poet does

- A modern poet strives not to be 'poetical', 'e'en' for the sake of rhythm or rhyme.
- We don't change the usual order of words.
- We don't use 'poetical' contractions such as: ne'er, e'en, 'tis, 'twas, o'er, 'twixt, 'neath.
- We don't put in a 'do' or 'did' where it wouldn't be used in normal speech. So, 'I cried' is fine, but 'I did cry' is OUT.
- 'Cut out all those exclamation marks. An exclamation mark is like laughing at your own joke' (F. Scott Fitzgerald).
- We don't use 'poetical' exclamations such as: O!, Oh! and Ah!
- We avoid words that don't occur in normal conversation. So: woe, befall, adieu, thee, thine, fain, etc. are all OUT.
- We avoid clichés and overworked phrases.
- We would rather write unrhymed poetry, or prose, than settle for second or third best words just to achieve a rhyme. The aim is that every word should be exactly the right one.
- We never pop in an extra word, or two, just to make the rhythm right. Every word in a poem must 'earn its keep'.
- Like a clown on a trapeze, knowing the rules, we might occasionally break them. This is also known as Mike Jubb's 'get-out' clause!

(Thanks to Colin Archer for these ideas.)

Appreciation and analysis

- Reading poetry out loud is the best way of appreciating its musical qualities and making it come alive.
- When you read a poem to children, think PERFORMANCE. Practise beforehand, making sure that you can read it with proper pace, timing and inflection.
- Putting on different voices may not come naturally to you but, if a poem calls for it, at least try a different pitch. After all, you do that when you're singing.
- Children often rush when reading aloud; **you** should err on the side of slowness, 'savour the flavour'. (See *A Poetry Teacher's Toolkit* Book 4, Ch. 4.)
- If you can perform poetry well, no child will ever leave your class not liking poetry . . . despite what some children may **say**.
- In a 10- or 15-minute session, read the poem once, and then ask the children to listen for something specific, such as an example of alliteration or a metaphor, during a second reading. Finish with a third reading.
- If you take up the 'Poem of the Week' idea, try to read it aloud several times during the week, highlighting a different aspect each time.
- The words 'analysis' and 'appreciation' sound boring, and may have connotations with indifferent poetry teaching during your own schooldays. These are require-ments of the National Literacy Strategy, but they don't **have** to be boring. Well taught, they are not.
- Poetry for children should firstly be for pleasure, and recognising the tricks of the

writer's trade can add to that pleasure. But, in a short session it's better to select just one technique than to dissect the poem totally.

The Internet

You will find quite a few references to the Internet throughout this book and the other volumes in the series. If you haven't discovered surfing the World Wide Web with a purpose yet, there is a vast amount of free information, ideas and lesson plans out there just waiting for you.

1 Good Form!

Featured poems

Today's the Day by Celia Warren
Dreamer by Brian Moses
Haiku by Japanese Masters
Triad by Adelaide Crapsey
The Warning by Adelaide Crapsey
Daughter of the Sea by Philip Gross
After the Storm by William Wordsworth
There Was a Young Bard of Japan, Anon.
My Cat is Dead by Mike Jubb
Turn the Clock Back by Charlotte Jarvis

'A poem is never finished, only abandoned.' (Paul Valery, 1871–1945)

Putting pattern into poems

I suppose the word 'form' in poetry is usually thought to mean some kind of pattern. The essential point about pattern, of course, is that something is repeated. In a rhyming poem, it's the sound at the end of some of the lines.

But for children, a simpler, yet effective, way of putting a pattern into a poem is to build in some repetition at the **beginning** of lines. Brian Moses does this in his poem *Dreamer* (p. 41). By creating a formula for himself ('I dreamt I was . . . and . . .'), he ensures that the piece will have both rhythm and unity. OK, in this case the final sound of each couplet is 'ee', but the poem would work just as well if they were all different.

WRITING ACTIVITY: I dreamt I was . . .

Using *Dreamer* as a model, get the children to write about some of the contents of a house. The poem could be called something like *Neglected.*

I dreamt I was a chair
but no-one sat on me.

I dreamt I was a cup
but no-one drank from me.

As with Brian's poem, restrict them to six items plus a concluding stanza. And you may think it prudent to tell the little darlings that the toilet (but not the bath) is out of bounds! What other areas could be explored using the 'I dreamt I was' formula?

WRITING ACTIVITY: Good/bad poems

This is another formula that can be used many times – I call it a good/bad poem. First, you decide what you want to write about: maybe Mum or Dad, brother or sister, or someone else you know. Or it could be something like cats or snow. Next, you think up some good things, and some not-so-good things, about your subject, and fit some of them into the pattern below.

Compose one at the board with the whole class first, then let them loose.

Cats

Cats are soft and furry, but
    they leave hairs on the sofa.
Cats are playful, but
    they dig their claws into you.
Cats are elegant, but
    they kill birds.

Cats are confusing.   M.J.

The formula can be played around with:

My Mum is . . . , but
sometimes she . . .

Coming up with three 'good' and three 'bad' things isn't too onerous, but more could get boring. I suggest to children that they come up with a 'tidy-up' or 'summing-up' line, which breaks the pattern, to end the poem, e.g. My cat, Rover, sleeps on the fridge.

Reading/collecting

Ask the children to search for, and copy out, non-rhyming poems that have repetition at the beginning of lines. The more they read and hear, the more they'll get the idea. Here's a little something dashed off by Amy Bulpitt of Peel Common Junior School, Gosport. It's simple, but effective.

My Mum
My mum loves me, My mum loves my dad,
My mum loves my brother, The only thing she
    Doesn't like is

        H A S S L E !

Here's one from Nathan Bethell, also of Peel Common Junior School, Gosport:

I love	*I HATE*
I love T.V.	I HATE T.V.
I love sport	I HATE sport
I HATE school	I love school
I HATE work	I love work
I love Pompey	I HATE Pompey
I love Liverpool	I HATE Liverpool

I love you and I love you

WRITING ACTIVITY: *More patterns*

Make up your own formulae for poems, and encourage children to do the same.

Other ideas for creating pattern at the start of lines: time of the day, days of the week, months of the year, seasons, counting up, counting down.

Haiku

'Haiku happen all the time, wherever there are people who are 'in touch' with the world of their senses, and with their own feeling response to it.' (*The Haiku Handbook* by William J. Higginson)

'Haiku is the poetry of meaningful touch, taste, sound, sight and smell.' (R. H. Blyth)

Everyone knows that a haiku consists of three lines of five, seven and five syllables respectively. But, if you **really** want to find out about haiku, I thoroughly recommend *The Haiku Handbook* by William J. Higginson (ISBN 4–7700–1430–9). It's a fascinating and comprehensive eye-opener about this, and related, forms of Japanese poetry.

Here are two facts that I've learnt:

- Haiku is an **evolving** form, with its origins as the opening stanza of a collaborative poem called *renga* (linked poem) or *haikai-no-renga* (humorous renga).
- Japanese poets do **not** count syllables. If they bother counting anything at all, they count different sound units called *onji*. A Japanese haiku translates into something nearer 12 English syllables, or even fewer.

Conclusions

- To insist that haiku is fixed in the form of a 17-syllable poem in three lines of five, seven and five syllables, is a simplistic trap.
- If the haiku of Japanese masters doesn't translate into 17 English syllables, why should haiku written in English conform to that 'rule'?
- As the form is still evolving, we're free to add our tuppence worth.
- The 'spirit' of haiku is more important than **specific** rules.

Sorry if I've confused you. Like me, you were probably quite happy with the 5–7–5 pattern. Perhaps you're thinking 'So, what **is** a haiku if it doesn't have rules?' Well, it **does** have rules, but they are not written in stone. As a writer I have often chosen the 5–7–5 pattern because I like the discipline, the problem-solving quality. It gives me a frame and throws me back into words, forcing me to seek alternatives.

However, after reading William Higginson's book, and doing a bit of Internet research, I now have a much broader appreciation of what a haiku can be. I now think we should be helping children write a variety of haiku-like poems, **selecting our/their own rules**.

The following are 20 rules, from many more that I found on the Internet. You can't follow them all at the same time because some contradict each other. But, you can mix and match the ones you want to follow, or make up your own. When you get fed up with one set of rules, choose some different ones.

1. 17 syllables written in three lines.
2. 17 syllables written in three lines divided into 5–7–5.
3. Fewer than 17 syllables written in three lines as short–long–short.
4. Use two images (see below).
5. Use three images.
6. Use a seasonal reference.
7. Just write about ordinary things.
8. Use only images from nature. No mention of people.
9. Mix people and nature.
10. Never have all three lines make a complete or run-on sentence. There must be a caesura (break) at the end of the first **or** the second line (see below).
11. Always write in the present tense.
12. Use normal punctuation.
13. Use no punctuation.
14. All words in lower case.
15. All words in upper case.
16. No rhymes.
17. Rhyme the last words of the first and third lines.
18. Use alliteration.
19. Save the punchline for the last line.
20. Use no verbs.

The **essence** of haiku is here-and-now experience, and image. For this reason, it doesn't use such literary devices as metaphor or personification, which would detract from the 'nowness'. Alliteration and onomatopoeia can be used, however. The **purpose** of haiku is to capture the moment and to share it; to try to get the reader or listener to feel what **we** are feeling. This is attempted not so much through description, but through simple presentation of images. It is much stronger writing to **show** an image of your loneliness than it is simply to **tell** the reader that you were feeling lonely. (For more about 'show don't tell' see *A Poetry Teacher's Toolkit* Book 4, Ch. 1.)

Therefore, before children can write effective haiku, they need to understand the concept of 'an image' which, in this context, refers to any of our senses, not just the visual:

the last leaf on a tree; the smell from a chip shop; distant sirens in the night; a chocolate liqueur when you bite into it; being licked by a puppy.

An image is **any** sensory snapshot. It 'rings a bell' in our **imag**ination. It evokes a sensory response, or an emotion, by dipping into our memory banks; it doesn't **tell** us what to feel. Here are some more:

> a wonky supermarket trolley; body odour; the daytime moon; burnt toast; a dead bird on a beach; people laughing after you've walked by; a wedding ring in the gutter; having your hair ruffled; a glove on a fence; your mum's perfume; an old lady trying to cross a busy road; a broken doll; snow down your back; two robins fighting; exhaust from a diesel lorry; a statue of Queen Victoria; having an injection.

The very best way to get children to absorb the idea of 'image' is to read them many examples of good haiku. If you read 20, slowly, one after another with a few seconds pause between each, it would take less than five minutes. Then, if you tell the children that the poems contain images ('So what do you think an image is?'), the subsequent discussion can bring out ideas such as 'pictures in your head' and 'imagination' (which almost includes the word 'image').

 ## WRITING ACTIVITY: Recording images

Once they've got the idea, persuade the children to start their own collection of images. A page in their draft book could be set aside for this, so that the images don't have to be used immediately. Jotting down material for future use is a good habit to acquire. Brevity is important, so give them an initial limit of, say, ten words per image, but fewer if they can. They don't need to write, 'I saw a . . . ' or 'I heard some . . . ' – just the image itself.

Impress upon the children the importance of using **all** their senses, and of being alert for images everywhere: at home, on TV, in the park, in the supermarket, on the way to school, in the school grounds. Images can also come from their memory (when Dad tripped over the dog), and from fantasy (I'm riding Pegasus).

When it comes to the actual composing of haiku, it's only a matter of practice to turn an image – or probably a combination of two images – into a scenario. Remember to emphasise that there is no room for superfluous words in haiku. And the layout is a matter of personal choice.

> a child's glove in a puddle;
> an old man hangs it
> on his broken fence

It has 17 syllables, but I'm not going to set it out like this:

a child's glove in a
puddle an old man hangs it
on his broken fence

And I'm certainly not going to write:

child's glove in puddle

just to conform to the fallacious Western interpretation of what a 'proper' haiku is.
A 'corollary' of that particular haiku could be:

late for school
on a freezing day;
only one glove

I hope I've persuaded you that always to stick to 5–7–5 is really a nonsense for our children. What is more important: getting them to write effective images or counting syllables? And the same goes for tanka.
Combining two images can often result in one plus one equals three:

Image 1: a cat looking out of the window

Image 2: birds on a bird table

cat behind glass;
a sparrow on the bird table
eats biscuit crumbs   M.J.

This works (I think) because we can all 'sense' the cat's frustration at not being able to get at the sparrow. It's the **juxtaposition** of two images that adds the extra dimension. Note how line two 'runs into' line three.
The **caesura** is the break or pause at the end of the first line, denoted above by a semi-colon. A caesura can be placed at the end of the second line, or both, or even in the middle of a line. I'm very keen that the 'rule' of having at least one caesura should be kept to; it seems to me part of the essence of haiku not to have a single run-on sentence.
Here's a second version of the above haiku that I prefer.

cat behind glass;
on the bird table
a sparrow takes the biscuit   M.J.

Using the idiom 'taking the biscuit' creates a double meaning. And I hope there's an element of humour injected with the sense that the sparrow is taunting the cat.

In this version, there is a 'natural' caesura at the end of line two; the line break does the job of a comma, so no other punctuation is necessary.

Linking two images picked at random can be fun, and creative. You'll have to take my word for it that the following began as random selections.

Image 1: a glove on a fence

Image 2: a statue of Queen Victoria

>snow melting
>from Queen Victoria;
>a glove on the railings   M.J.

'But what does it mean?', children might ask. Answer: It doesn't have to **mean** anything. It aims to take the **direct** route to the reader's senses, bypassing meaning to arrive at feelings. Or, you could say that it means what you want it to mean.

Setting 'em up to knock 'em down is a good angle.

>July shade . . .
>picnicking by the woods
>when bulldozers arrive

Another variation is to have the first two lines about nature, and the third totally unconnected.

>a field of buttercups;
>clouds turning pink . . .

>I've left the oven on

I am not saying that these are great haiku – but we would be pleased if the kids in our class wrote them. They can. And if they write loads of them, the rest of their creative writing will benefit too.

Haiku by Buson (p. 42)

>evening breeze . . .
>water laps the legs
>of the blue heron

Just to ram the syllable message home, this Japanese poem translates into 3–5–5 syllables; but, according to the purists, if I had written:

> spring shower . . .
> rain tickles the toes
> of the grey wagtail

it wouldn't be a haiku. Eyewash!

Does the Buson poem consist of two or three images? Certainly, there's the evening breeze, and the blue heron standing in shallow water that is lapping round its legs. But, because the second line ends with the word 'legs', I think there's a fraction of time when we don't know whose legs are being lapped. So, there's a slight surprise there – it might have turned out to be a pink dragon.

Whether it's two or three images, the combination adds up to more than the separate parts. For instance, what time of year is it? I visualise summer, because the heron is still fishing so it must be a light evening. The caesura in this poem is at the end of line one and is denoted by the common device of a row of dots. A colon, semi-colon or dash can be used, but many writers prefer to use no punctuation at all, relying on the words themselves to denote where the caesura is . . . as here:

Haiku by Buson (p. 42)

> a thief
> vanishes over the rooftops
> night chill

The syllable count here is 2–8–2 and, with no punctuation, the caesura falls at the end of the second line; you can't fail to pause there. This poem is another good example of how image builds on image – not until you read 'night chill' does it all come together and you 'see' (at least I do) a dark shape against the sky. The word 'chill' somehow refers not only to the temperature, but also to the fact that you've witnessed something chilling.

Go surfing for 'haiku' on the Internet. There's loads of free stuff, put there by generous people who just want to share their enthusiasm.

Tanka (meaning 'short poem')

Tanka has a **typical** form of 5–7–5–7–7 onji/syllables and is the grandmother of haiku. Tanka has a history of about 13 centuries as opposed to about three centuries for haiku. It is, therefore, **not** based on the haiku as stated in the National Literacy Strategy document.

As with haiku, you can approach tanka very simplistically: 5–7–5–7–7, and that's it. Or you can get bogged down in complications and controversy. What I am trying to do is to find a middle way that is appropriate for English-speaking children. But, when it comes down to it, it's a matter of personal taste as to which 'rules' are adopted.

Similarities with haiku

Simplicity and succinctness, traditionally reflecting nature with no violence or war images.

Some differences

- tanka are lyrical, haiku are fragmented;
- tanka speak of beauty, haiku try to capture 'is-ness' or presence;
- tanka have contemplation, haiku are quick and direct;
- tanka have emotion, haiku aim to have no **stated** emotion;
- tanka use imagination, haiku use senses with concrete images.

The only way really to get into the difference between these two forms is to read as many of each as possible, both modern and by the Japanese masters.

Rensaku ('linked work')

A longer work composed of individual haiku or tanka which function as stanzas of the whole, and are not independent.

> silent nightingale,
> the cage that you occupy
> is not the whole world
>
> sad, lonely songbird,
> treated like a clockwork toy . . .
> sing inside your head
>
> no consolation:
> the emperor too is trapped
> with no song to sing   M.J.

The writing principle 'show, don't tell' (referred to earlier) suggests that I shouldn't be **telling** the reader that the nightingale is sad and lonely. So I may change this one yet. (For more about 'show, don't tell' see *A Poetry Teacher's Toolkit* Book 4, Ch. 1.)

Gunsaku ('group work')

A group of haiku or tanka on a single subject which illuminates the subject from various points of view, but can be read independently, e.g. a group of children could tackle the subject of 'Winter' by sharing out combinations of the following aspects: weather, animal hibernation, migration, difficulties for birds and animals, deciduous trees, conifers, a festival, colour, day length, etc. (see Chapter 4 for a strategy for brainstorming).

Cinquains

In about 1909/10, American poet Adelaide Crapsey was inspired by Japanese poetry to devise the cinquain. This has a total of 22 syllables, in five lines of two, four, six, eight and two syllables respectively. I'm not inspired by this form but, unlike haiku, maybe we should adhere to the syllable constraint because that's the way it was created. However, this form is also still evolving, making it a good one for children to experiment with. For instance, I found one site for children on the Internet that had cinquains as being 2–4–6–8–2 **words** (not syllables) respectively.

Images remain important in the cinquain, but the two reproduced examples by Adelaide Crapsey show that opinion and interpretation are 'allowed' in a way that shouldn't happen in haiku.

The Warning by Adelaide Crapsey (p. 43)

Written as a haiku, this poem might be:

> still dusk . . .
> a white moth –
> I shiver

The aim is to present, or show, the experience. (For more about 'show, don't tell' see *A Poetry Teacher's Toolkit* Book 4, Ch. 1.)

Crapsey's cinquain, however, **tells** the reader, e.g. by the inclusion of the second adjective, 'strange'. The final sentence, 'Why am I grown / So cold?' is more blatantly linked to the white moth and is perhaps more akin to the phrase 'somebody just walked on my grave' than my haiku effort. Again, to a lover of haiku, the word 'flew' is unnecessary – unless you're counting syllables of course.

Poems using kennings

A kenning is a compound expression which originated in Old English and Norse poetry. It's a specialised kind of metaphor, often of two words, which describes something according to its attributes. In the Norse, a ship became an 'oar steed'. A kenning is, therefore, not a poem in itself, but a fuller word-picture of something can be created by combining a number of kennings.

Daughter of the Sea by Philip Gross (p. 44)

In this poem, Philip Gross invents many kennings to portray the changing character of a river as it flows from boggy source to embracing sea.

Ask the children what the rhyming pattern is. I had read the poem several times before I clicked that, for example, 'leaper' in the second stanza continues the rhymes of stanza one. Similarly, 'pusher' in stanza three harks back to the second stanza (near-rhyme); and so on. Is it too fanciful to say that the rhymes 'flow' from one stanza into the next? For the first three stanzas, the stream increases in power until, in stanza four, it enters a 'still pool'. The line 'don't be fooled' echoes the saying 'still waters run deep' in my mind.

Stanza five is brilliant. In nine words, Philip Gross shows the sight and sound of a roaring waterfall. Note the near-rhyme of 'fall' with 'pool/fooled/cool', and the terrific internal rhyme of 'thunder under'. Other near-rhymes: 'lunger/plunger/**under**/**mind her**'; 'binner/**in her**/dinner/skinner'; 'porter/water/daughter/**caught her**'.

Examples of alliteration: 'foam flicker', 'pebble pusher', 'keeping cool', 'leap lunger', 'dog's dinner', 'weary water', 'long lost'. Examples of assonance: 'bog/moss', 'trickle/swish', 'leap/free'.

The phrase 'long lost daughter of the sea' should be read without a pause, followed by 'the sea', and then 'the sea/has caught her up in its arms and set her free'. Never let punctuation or line breaks get in the way of meaning.

Rather than just ask kids to think up kennings, it's best to get them to brainstorm, or research in the library, first.

Badger: boar, sow, stripey, dig, claws, sett, underground, tunnels, woods, nocturnal, night, earthworms, insects, roots, fruits, cubs, etc.

Then, it is just a question of experimenting.

Stripey face
Sharp claws
Tunnel digger
Sett dweller
Night feeder
Worm chewer
Day sleeper
Snore boar   M.J.

It's funny how things come round; we used to call combs 'bug-rakes' when I was at school . . . 30 years before I heard the word 'kenning'. (See also the section on 'compound words' in *A Poetry Teacher's Toolkit* Book 4, Ch. 3.)

Acrostics

If you have been away somewhere, and don't know what an acrostic is, look it up in the glossary of the National Literacy Strategy (see also the Glossary at the end of this volume).

Brock meets brock
After dark,
Digging around for
Grubs and
Earthworms;
Rummaging
Stripes in the night   M.J.

A very basic acrostic would have just one word on each line. But, they can be more sophisticated.

> **B**rock meets brock in a Wiltshire wood
> **A**fter dark, to forage for food;
> **D**igging around for a bite to eat:
> **G**rubs and other tasty treats.
> **E**arthworms are their choice delight.
> **R**ummaging raiders; with black and white
> **S**tripes in the night. Stripes in the night.   M.J.

Alphabets: poems based on alphabetical order

 WRITING ACTIVITY: Write an alphabet poem

This can be used as a model.

Doughnuts

I like doughnuts.

I like:
Apple doughnuts
Banana doughnuts
Curry doughnuts
Double-decker doughnuts
Eggy doughnuts
Fizzy doughnuts
Gobstopper doughnuts
Hot cross doughnuts
Ice-cream doughnuts
Jelly doughnuts
King-size doughnuts
Liquorice doughnuts
Macaroni doughnuts
Nutty doughnuts
Onion doughnuts
Pickled doughnuts
Queen-size doughnuts
Rhubarb doughnuts
Salt and vinegar doughnuts

Toad-in-the-doughnut
Upside-down doughnuts
Vanilla doughnuts
Watercress doughnuts
eXtra jammy doughnuts (well what can you do?)
Yoghurt doughnuts

AND

Zero doughnuts.
(They're the ones with the hole in the middle.)   M.J.

Or for the really ambitious:

Supposed encounter of the alphabetical kind

Alien **B**eings
Cunningly **D**escended **E**arthwards
From **G**alactic **H**oles
In **J**et-**K**inetic-**L**aser
Masterships.

Not **O**ffering **P**eace.

Quarrelsome **R**eptiles!

Savagely,
They **U**sed **V**aporising **W**eapons:

X-**Y**onkers.

ZAP ! ! !   M.J.

Limericks

These need no explanation really, but, for the sake of good form (pun intended), it's a five-line poem with an AABBA rhyming scheme, and a 'dee DUM diddy DUM diddy DUM' rhythm. Here's one with my compliments:

> An overworked teacher called Beth
> Sadly died when she ran out of breath;
> But she's making the most
> Of being a ghost
> By scaring the children to death.   M.J.

Work on rhythm and syllables earlier in this volume (and in *A Poetry Teacher's Toolkit* Book 1 and Book 2), should help children to readjust their first thoughts in order to fit the desired pattern.

THE LITERACY HOUR: YEARS 3 AND 4

National Literacy Strategy objectives: Years 3 and 4

Year 3
- To express their views about a . . . poem identifying specific words or phrases to support their viewpoint.
- To experiment with deleting words in sentences to see which are essential to retaining meaning and which are not.
- To infer the meaning of unknown words from context.

Year 4
- To identify different patterns of rhyme and verse in poetry.
- To reread own writing to check for grammatical sense and accuracy.
- To define familiar vocabulary in their own words.

Chosen poem

Today's the Day by Celia Warren (p. 39)

Materials needed

Board or flipchart
Marker pens
Copies of the chosen poem (see 'Preparation')
Activity sheets (see 'Preparation')
Dictionaries
Scissors
Pens, pencils, writing paper/books
Letter tiles
'Feely' bag

Preparation

Make three enlarged copies of the chosen poem.
    Make copies of the poem for each child in Group 1.
    Make copies of the activity sheets for each child, according to achievement level (photocopiable sheets 1a, 1b, 1c on pp. 33–35).

Take out the letters 'q', 'v', 'x', 'y' and 'z' from the set of letter tiles. Put the remaining letters in the feely bag.

With the whole class

- Tell the children what the title of the poem is and ask what they think it might be about. Today's the day for what? Write key words on the board linked to their ideas.
- Share the poem, letting the children follow the text as you read. When you have finished, ask them what the poem is about. Look at the key words written at the beginning of the session from their suggestions. How accurate were their guesses?
- Ask the children whether there is a rhyming pattern to the poem. Can they say what it is? (ABAB) Do they notice any other pattern within the poem? Point out that the second line of each verse becomes the first line of the following verse, and that the last line of each verse becomes the third line of the following verse, sometimes with a slight variation.
- Challenge the children to tell you the link between the final and the first verses. If necessary, show them how these verses continue the pattern already explored and in this way make the poem 'circular'. Ask them what they think of this device and why. Explain that a poem which does this is called a pantoum, a form originally from Malaysia (see Glossary and Further Reading).
- Focus on some of the words that may be unfamiliar to the children. For example, 'abstinence', 'meditate', 'Domestic', 'chores' or '(poetic) grist'. Encourage them to use the context of the verse in particular, and the poem in general, to work out the meanings of the words. Write their suggested definitions on the board and ask a volunteer to check the words in the dictionary.
- Using the three enlarged copies, explore the poem in the following ways:
  1. Ask different children to come out and draw a circle around any lines that are repeated using different coloured marker pens for each 'set' of repeats. How often is any one line written? (Twice)
  2. Ask different children to delete any repeated line that is in the poem. Read the lines that are left as four-line verses. Ask the children what has happened to the rhyming pattern. (Apart from the first verse, which stays intact and remains ABAB, the 'new pattern' is AABB.) What has happened to the link between the first and final verses? Which version do the children prefer? Why?
  3. Ask different children to come out and delete all lines that are repeated anywhere in the poem. What is left when they have finished? (Nothing!) What do they think about this? Encourage them to give reasons for their answers.
- If the children could choose a day not to do something they usually have to, what would they do instead? List their ideas on the board and leave these up for the group session.

Group and independent work (differentiated groups)

Group 1

Give each child a copy of the poem and a pair of scissors. Ask the children to cut the poem into its separate verses and experiment with these to see if they can make another poem. Tell them they could discard some verses if it helps them to create a more sensible piece of work. (This activity could also be done in pairs or as a group, according to achievement level.) They should write out their new poem.

Group 2

Give out copies of the activity sheets 1a (for lower achievers), 1b (for average achievers) and 1c (for higher achievers) and ask the children to complete them.

Group 3

Working closely with the children, allocate two or three lines (not consecutive) to each child to learn. Help them to recite the poem by speaking their lines at the correct point. When they are confident enough, they could make up some actions to go with their lines. Let them give a class performance when they are ready.

Group 4

Ask the children to work together to draft a group poem about what they would do on a 'chosen day off'. They should use the ideas written on the board at the end of the whole-class session for support. Remind them that their poem doesn't have to rhyme and they should not try to make it as long as Celia Warren's – a shorter, better poem is preferable to a longer, poorer effort. ('Never mind the length – look at the quality'!) Encourage them to draft and redraft before agreeing the final version. (This activity could be done individually if preferred.)

Group 5

Give the group the feely bag containing the letter tiles. Ask the children to write an alphabet poem about *Doughnuts* (see activity above, p. 24). They should take out several letters from the feely bag (the number according to achievement level), put these into alphabetical order and use them as the first letters of the lines of their poems.

Plenary session (whole class)

- Ask the group that learnt the poem to give a class performance if they are ready.
- Ask volunteers to tell you the rhyming pattern and verse pattern of *Today's the Day*.
- Share the poem once again, encouraging the children to join in.
- Did they enjoy exploring this poem? Can they say why or why not?

THE LITERACY HOUR: YEARS 5 AND 6

National Literacy Strategy objectives: Years 5 and 6

Year 5
- To use the structures of poems read to write extensions based on these.
- To discuss, proofread and edit their own writing for clarity and correctness.
- To use a range of dictionaries and understand their purposes.

Year 6
- To analyse how messages, moods, feelings and attitudes are conveyed in poetry.
- To have awareness of the conventions of standard English.
- To use dictionaries and IT spell checks.

Chosen poem

Dreamer by Brian Moses (p. 41)

Materials needed

Flipchart or board
Marker pens
Enlarged copy of the chosen poem (see 'Preparation')
Copies of the chosen poem for Group 2 (see 'Preparation')
Activity sheets (see 'Preparation')
Card for 'environment cards' (see 'Preparation')
Cassette recorder/player and blank cassette
Dictionaries and thesauruses
Pens, pencils, writing paper/books
Variety of musical instruments – percussion, wind, etc.

Preparation

On the flipchart write the title *Imagination* and the beginning of three verses,

> *I imagined I was a*
> *And I*

Cover the page until later in the whole-class session.
   Make an enlarged copy of the chosen poem.
   On an A4 copy of the poem, blank out the second line of each verse except for 'and'.
Make a copy for each child in Group 2.

Make copies of the activity sheets for each child, according to achievement level (photocopiable sheets 1aa, 1bb, 1cc on pp. 36–38).

Make a set of cards, each with a word written on it, connected with the environment or natural world. For example, 'bird', 'sea', 'butterflies' and so on. You should make at least three different cards for each child in Group 4.

With the whole class

- Show the title of the poem to the children and ask them to guess what the poem might be about. Explain that it was written by Brian Moses and he wanted to use his poem to talk about the way the world is being treated.

- Share the poem with the children letting them see the text as you read. When you have finished, ask the children what Brian Moses wants to say in his poem? How does he think we are treating the world? Is he happy or comfortable with what is happening? How do they know? Encourage them to tell you words or phrases from the poem that support their answers.

- Can the children see a rhyming pattern in the poem? Show how the final word of the first four verses is 'me', and the final word of the last three verses uses rhyme and near-rhyme to tie up with the other verses – the 'y' of 'ivory', 'trees' and 'see'.

- Ask the children to tell you the verse pattern of the poem (two-line verses or couplets; each verse, except the last, beginning with 'I dreamt I was a/an . . .'; the second line beginning with 'and no . . .').

- How is the final verse different from the others? (It has three lines instead of two; the first line reads 'I dreamt I painted . . .' instead of 'I dreamt I was . . .'; there is a completely different second line; there is no implication of negative actions.) Can the children suggest why the final verse is different from the others?

- Tell the children you're all going to write a poem in the style of *Dreamer*, but it will be called *Imagination*. Uncover the page where you wrote the beginning of the new poem and ask a volunteer to read what you have written. Brainstorm ideas for the poem. You could give them a start with an example such as,

I imagined I was a bird
And I couldn't sing

- Discuss ideas and redraft until you have a version agreed by most of the class. Leave the final version on the board.

Group and independent work (differentiated groups)

Group 1
(This activity may have to be done away from the main classroom.) Work with the children and use the musical instruments to accompany *Dreamer* while it is being recited. Encourage them to choose appropriate instruments, rhythms and volumes for each verse. For example, they could use percussion played loudly and fast in the 'whale' verse, or a gently and slowly played wind instrument for the 'stream' verse.

Practise the accompaniment and the poem's recital together until everyone in the group is satisfied with their work.

Group 2
Give out the blanked-off copies of the poem and some dictionaries and thesauruses. Ask the children to complete each verse with a rewritten second line. Tell them they should use the dictionaries and thesauruses to help them find alternative words. Let them refer to the original poem to jog their memories. They could work in pairs for support.

Group 3
Give out copies of the activity sheets 1aa (for lower achievers), 1bb (for average achievers) and 1cc (for higher achievers) and ask the children to complete them. Encourage them to use the thesauruses and dictionaries.

Group 4
Put the shuffled 'environment' cards face down on the table and give the children the cassette recorder/player and blank cassette. They should each take a card in turn, read the word written on it and then decide a verse in the style of *Dreamer*. For example, if they took 'butterfly', they could say 'I dreamt I was a butterfly and nobody caught me in a net'. When they have finalised their verses, the children should put them together and record them onto the cassette, to make a group poem.

Group 5
Ask the children to choose one of the natural things from Brian Moses' poem *Dreamer*, for example 'forest', 'whale', etc. They should then write the word vertically and write a poem in acrostic form (see activity above, p. 24). They could do this activity in pairs for support.

Plenary session (whole class)

- Share the poem once again, encouraging the children to join in with you and asking Group 1 to play their instrumental accompaniment.
- Discuss whether Brian Moses' poem made the children think about environmental issues. Encourage them to say why or why not. Do they like poems that tackle important topics? Why or why not?

SHEET 1a

Name _____

Read *Today's the Day* by Celia Warren.

Complete this poem in the style of *Today's the Day*. Remember – your poem doesn't have to rhyme. You could use the words at the bottom to help.

Today

Today, I've decided not to _____

Instead I'm going to _____ or _____

My _____ have been put away

So the fun of my day off will not be spoilt.

Instead I'm going to _____ or _____

I'm going to have a free day off!

The fun of my day off will not be spoilt and

I'll do some _____ instead.

clean my shoes   mend my bike   play some games

brush and polish   do my chores   visit John   play CDs

broom and duster   good computer games   wheelies on my bike

speedo scooter tricks

Use a dictionary to find the meanings of these words:

poetic _____

chores _____

SHEET 1b

Name _____

Read *Today's the Day* by Celia Warren.

Complete this poem in the style of *Today's the Day*. Remember – your poem doesn't have to rhyme. You could use the words at the bottom to help, or you could make up your own.

Today

Today, I've decided not to _____

Instead I'm going to _____ or _____

My _____ have been put away

So the fun of my day off will not be spoilt.

Instead I'm going to _____ or _____

I'm going to have a free day off!

The fun of my day off will not be spoilt and

I'll do some _____ instead.

clean my shoes   play some games   do my chores   play CDs

broom and duster   wheelies on my bike   speedo scooter tricks

Use a dictionary to find the meanings of these words:

domestic _____

chores _____

meditate _____

grist _____

© Collette Drifte and Mike Jubb (2002) *A Poetry Teacher's Toolkit*, Book 3. London: David Fulton Publishers.

SHEET 1c

Name _____

Read *Today's the Day* by Celia Warren.

Complete this poem in the style of *Today's the Day*. Remember – your poem doesn't have to rhyme. The first two verses have been set for you. Write a third verse yourself.

Today

Today, I've decided not to _____
Instead I'm going to _____ or _____
My _____ have been put away
So the fun of my day off will not be spoilt.

Instead I'm going to _____ or _____
I'm going to have a free day off!
The fun of my day off will not be spoilt and
I'll do some _____ instead.

_____

_____

_____

_____

Use a dictionary to find the meanings of these words:

domestic _____

chores _____

meditate _____

grist _____

abstinence _____

creative _____

SHEET 1aa

Name _____

Read *Dreamer* by Brian Moses.

Complete this poem in the style of *Dreamer*. Remember – your poem doesn't have to rhyme. You could use the words at the bottom to help.

Thinking

I thought I was an ocean
and someone _____ me.

I thought I was the sky
and someone _____ me.

I thought I was a tiger
and someone _____ me.

polluted   dirtied   hunted   poisoned

Use a thesaurus to find synonyms for these words:

hunter _____

_____

stream _____

_____

smile _____

_____

SHEET 1bb

Name _____

Read *Dreamer* by Brian Moses.

Complete this poem in the style of *Dreamer*. Remember – your poem doesn't have to rhyme.

Thinking

I thought I was a river
and someone _____ me.

I thought I was a rhino
and someone _____ me.

I thought I was the sea
and someone _____ me.

Use a thesaurus to find synonyms for these words:

poison_____

_____

forest _____

_____

air _____

_____

painted _____

_____

SHEET 1cc

Name _____

Read *Dreamer* by Brian Moses.

Complete this poem in the style of *Dreamer*. Remember – your poem doesn't have to rhyme. The first two verses have been set for you. Write a third verse yourself.

Thinking

I thought I was a _____
and someone _____ me.

I thought _____
and _____

_____
_____.

Use a thesaurus to find synonyms for these words:

ocean _____   pollute _____
_____   _____

blacken _____   Earth _____
_____   _____

face _____   ivory _____
_____   _____

© Collette Drifte and Mike Jubb (2002) *A Poetry Teacher's Toolkit*, Book 3. London: David Fulton Publishers.

Today's the Day

Celia Warren

Today's the day I've chosen not to write.
I'll decorate the house. I'll cut the grass.
All my pens are tidied out of sight
In case this phase of abstinence should pass.

I'll decorate the house. I'll cut the grass.
I'll do what other wives and mothers do.
Before this phase of abstinence can pass
Perhaps I'll bake a cake or cook a stew.

I'll do what other wives and mothers do.
The basketful of ironing will get done.
Perhaps I'll bake a cake or cook a stew.
Keeping house is really rather fun.

The basketful of ironing will get done.
It gives me time to meditate and think.
Keeping house is really rather fun.
It's quite creative polishing a sink.

It gives me time to meditate and think
Of all the things that I might write about.
It's quite creative polishing a sink.
Housework has its moments, there's no doubt.

Today's the Day (continued)

Of all the things that I might write about
Domestic chores are low down on the list.
But housework has its moments, there's no doubt
A vacuum cleaner has poetic grist.

Domestic chores are low down on the list.
Yet, today's the day I've chosen not to write
'A vacuum cleaner has poetic grist'.
And all my pens are tidied out of sight.

Dreamer

Brian Moses

I dreamt I was an ocean
and no one polluted me.

I dreamt I was a whale
and no hunters came after me.

I dreamt I was the air
and nothing blackened me.

I dreamt I was a stream
and nobody poisoned me.

I dreamt I was an elephant
and nobody stole my ivory.

I dreamt I was a rain forest
and no one cut down my trees.

I dreamt I painted a smile
on the face of the Earth
for all to see.

Haiku

Japanese Masters

old pond . . .
a frog leaps in
water's sound   (Basho, 1644–1694)

well! let's go
snow-viewing till
we tumble (Basho)

evening breeze . . .
water laps the legs
of the blue heron   (Buson, 1716–1784)

a thief
vanishes over the rooftops
night chill   (Buson)

the coolness
the half-moon shifts
puddles   (Issa, 1762–1826)

summer river . . .
there's a bridge, but the horse
goes through water   (Shiki, 1867–1902)

autumn clear –
the smoke of something
goes into the sky   (Shiki)

Triad

Adelaide Crapsey

These be
Three silent things:
The falling snow . . . the hour
Before the dawn . . . the mouth of one
Just dead.

The Warning

Adelaide Crapsey

Just now,
Out of the strange
Still dusk . . . as strange, as still . . .
A white moth flew. Why am I grown
So cold?

Daughter of the Sea

Philip Gross

bog seeper
moss creeper
growing restless   getting steeper

trickle husher
swish and rusher
stone leaper   splash and gusher

foam flicker
mirror slicker
pebble pusher   boulder kicker

still pool
don't be fooled
shadow tricker   keeping cool

leap lunger
crash plunger
free fall   with thunder under

garbage binner
dump it in her
never mind her   dog's dinner

plastic bagger
old lagger
oil skinner   wharf nagger

Daughter of the Sea **(continued)**

cargo porter
weary water
tide dragger   long lost daughter

of the sea
the sea the sea
has caught her   up in its arms and set her free.

After the Storm

William Wordsworth

There was a roaring in the wind all night;
The rain came heavily and fell in floods;
But now the sun is rising calm and bright;
The birds are singing in the distant woods;
Over his own sweet voice the Stock-dove broods;
The Jay makes answer as the Magpie chatters;
And all the air is filled with pleasant noise of waters.

All things that love the sun are out of doors;
The sky rejoices in the morning's birth;
The grass is bright with raindrops; on the moors
The hare is running races in her mirth;
And with her feet she from the plashy earth
Raises a mist; that, glittering in the sun,
Runs with her all the way, wherever she doth run.

There Was a Young Bard of Japan

Anon.

There was a young bard of Japan,
Whose limericks never would scan;
   When told it was so,
   He said: 'Yes, I know,
But I always try to get as many words
into the last line as I possibly can.'

My Cat is Dead

Mike Jubb

My cat is dead. I have no cat,
though the catflap is still in the door.
It's very important you understand this:
I don't have a cat any more.

She died just over a year ago;
it was simply old age, said the vet.
But I'm terrified now to admit what I fear:
I'm haunted by my old pet.

It started about a week ago;
goose pimples covered my skin
when the catflap opened, and then swung shut,
but nothing was seen to come in.

Outside, it was raining and blowing a gale;
did the howling wind rattle the door?
My question was answered before I could speak,
as pawprints appeared on the floor.

I seemed to be stuck, with my mouth open wide;
the memory still torments me.
Before I could move, or think what to do,
some hidden thing rubbed up against me.

Every last part of me wanted to run,
but my feet were fixed to the floor.
I'm not a brave man, and I shook with fear
when I felt the scratch of a claw.

My Cat is Dead (continued)

I'm starting to get used to it now:
the miaows inside my . . .
excuse me, but I have to go;
she's calling me to be fed.

Turn the Clock Back

Charlotte Jarvis

(Rupert House School, Henley-on-Thames)

How can you cure his deafness?
Turn the clock back
To just before the bomb
Exploded beside him, bursting his eardrums.

How can you cure his blindness?
Turn the clock back
To just before the shrapnel
Pierced his eyes, darkening his world forever.

How can you cure his missing legs?
Turn the clock back
To just before the flames
Charred his skin, in pain forever.

How can you cure his mind?
Turn the clock back
To just before the explosions
Which hit his friends, killing his sanity.

How can you cure War?
Turn the clock back
To just before tempers became too hot
Smashing the peace, destroying humanity.

2 But is it Poetry?

Featured poems

Propper English by Alan F. G. Lewis
In the Wood by Sheila Simmons
The Dismantled Ship by Walt Whitman
The Ship Starting by Walt Whitman
Vesuvius by Mike and Nicky Jubb
Two Sisters by Mike Jubb
Earth Apples by Gerard Benson
Midnight Meeting by Mike Jubb

Boswell: 'Then, Sir, what is poetry?'
Johnson: 'Why, Sir, it is much easier to say what it is not. We all **know** what light
           is; but it is not easy to **tell** what it is.'

Poetry?

A few words
                    flung
          anyhow
          at the
                    page
like a handful
        of
        sticky sweets
and they call it a
     poem   M.J.

'I gave up on new poetry myself many years ago, when most of it began to read
like coded messages passing between lonely aliens on a hostile world.' (Russell
Baker)

Coleridge said that poetry is 'the best words in the best order'. And according to Robert Frost, 'Poetry is a way of taking life by the throat.' For me, the only definition of poetry that works every time is this: If the writer **says** it's a poem, then it's a poem. I know that many people will find that unsatisfactory but does it really matter? All **we're** trying to do is help children to explore poetry, and to write creatively. So let the precious people debate whether elbows are straight or crooked . . . we'll just get on with the practical stuff.

There are, however, some features that point to the differences between poetry and prose:

- In poetry, you don't have to start at the left-hand margin and continue until you reach the right-hand margin. Layout is a feature. Line breaks are a form of punctuation.
- In poetry, you don't have to write in 'proper' sentences. Some words carry more value than others; some of those 'others' may be expendable.
- Poetry doesn't have to have 'plot', or extended structure. It can be a single line about a passing thought.

Poetry, like the English language itself, is evolving. Trying to exclude anything that isn't 'traditional' is like a French academy trying to ban 'le weekend' from their language – they're beating up a deceased equine.

Free verse

'Writing free verse is like playing tennis with the net down.' (Robert Frost)

Just to distinguish between free verse and blank verse: in free verse, there are no set rules; blank verse is typically iambic pentameter that doesn't rhyme, much used by Shakespeare and Milton. The great thing about free verse, especially for children, is that nobody is entitled to tell you that you've got it wrong. How liberating that should be.

From my visits to schools, I know that there are still many children, and some adults, who think that poetry has to rhyme. Yet, many of the forms discussed in the previous chapter (haiku, tanka, cinquains, acrostics, alphabets, lists) don't rhyme. So why the hesitancy, even fear, over free verse?

I suspect the answer is that these other forms do at least have a structure or pattern that supports us in our writing. Free verse may not have that recognisable structure or pattern, but it still has form; in the same way that an abstract sculpture or painting has form. We may or may not like it, but I think fairness demands that we accept it as legitimate.

The idea of allowing the layout of a poem to be influenced by the flow of speech is the thinking behind the structure of free verse, although its history can be traced back at least to the King James Bible:

16   ¶ Then came there two women, that were harlots, unto the king, and stood before him.
17   And the one woman said, O my lord, I and this woman dwell in one house; and I was delivered of a child with her in the house.

18   And it came to pass the third day after that I was delivered, that this woman was delivered also: and we were together; there was no stranger with us in the house, save we two in the house.

19   And this woman's child died in the night; because she overlaid it.

20   And she arose at midnight, and took my son from beside me, while thine handmaid slept, and laid it in her bosom, and laid her dead child in my bosom.

21   And when I rose in the morning to give my child suck, behold, it was dead: but when I had considered it in the morning, behold, it was not my son, which I did bear.

22   And the other woman said, Nay; but the living is my son, and the dead is thy son. And this said, No; but the dead is thy son, and the living is my son. Thus they spake before the king.

23   ¶ Then said the king, The one saith, This is my son that liveth, and thy son is the dead: and the other saith, Nay; but thy son is the dead, and my son is the living.

24   And the king said, Bring me a sword. And they brought a sword before the king.

25   And the king said, Divide the living child in two, and give half to the one, and half to the other.

26   Then spake the woman whose the living child was unto the king, for her bowels yearned upon her son, and she said, O my lord, give her the living child, and in no wise slay it. But the other said, Let it be neither mine nor thine, but divide it.

27   Then the king answered and said, Give her the living child, and in no wise slay it: she is the mother thereof.

28   And all Israel heard of the judgment which the king had judged; and they feared the king: for they saw that the wisdom of God was in him to do judgment.

You may consider this passage about the wisdom of Solomon to be prose but, like so much of the authorised version, its poetic quality is undeniable. As English evolved, the archaic vocabulary of 'poetic' language had to be left behind, and some poets chose also to abandon the old forms which accompanied it. The free verse of Walt Whitman, T. S. Eliot and William Carlos Williams, among many others, means that this form of poetry is traditional now.

The Dismantled Ship by Walt Whitman (p. 73)

This poem consists of one intricate sentence. It's a 'proper' one too, perfectly punctuated, which could easily be the first sentence in a novel about some seafaring adventurer. It **is** a poem because: of the way it's set out; it sounds like poetry; it has no plot, no 'beginning, middle and end' in the story sense; description builds on description to produce one overall image; Whitman said it was a poem.

The first three lines are actually in strict meter (iambic), after which the rhythm is free. No similes or metaphors are employed, with just the one use of alliteration ('disabled, done'), and one instance of half-rhyme ('rusting/mouldering'). Conventional wisdom is to keep adjectives to a minimum, yet this poem abounds with them, e.g. 'An old, dismasted, grey and batter'd ship'. But I don't think that any one of them is superfluous; they all add something to the greater image. Moral: 'rules' are there to be broken – if you're good enough.

In the Wood by Sheila Simmons (p. 72)

This is an excellent example of what can be achieved when the modern poet is freed from the constraints of meter and rhyme.

> 'We were playing hide and seek outside the wood, and it was my turn to hide. As soon as the others started counting, I raced into the wood to look for a good hiding place.'

or

> One, two, three, four,
> They've begun to count . . .
> I race into the wood to hide

The prose version is mine, and contains 35 words. Sheila's lines have, or imply, exactly the same information in 15 words. Not only that, but she uses the present tense to give a feel of immediacy, not so easy to handle in prose. The short lines, and the preponderance of monosyllabic words, heighten the sense of urgency.

The concentrated 15 words communicate more than the diluted 35.

The fast pace of the first stanza is maintained by beginning the next three lines with explosive verbs, two of which are onomatopoeic: 'Thump, Dive, Crash'. I feel that the word 'off' following 'Dive' is a mistake – without it we would be left with 'Thump down', 'Dive through' and 'Crash between'. Then, 'Crouch in a secret hollow' starts to put the brakes on and is followed by the single-word slow-down line 'Wait'.

The second stanza is one of crouching anticipation. It starts with an image. Not 'I can hear echoing "Cooeee's"', just the essential two words. Similarly with 'Laughter,/Crack of branches'. Then, the intrusive external sounds stop, the pace is finally stilled, and the focus of stanza three is on the immediate surroundings, with the implication that they are noticed by the writer for the first time.

Sheila Simmons uses personification of plants three times in this poem. In the first stanza, the brambles were 'snatching'. Now, in stanza three, 'Foxgloves rear up' and 'Fern-over fronds lay long hands on me', both of which have a hint of menace, along with 'Dragon-necked, with purple tongues'. But that sense of oppressiveness, accentuated by 'Stifling' and the annoying swarms of flies, is passed over as 'The wood falls quiet'.

Now, somehow, we are listening as hard as the writer is. She becomes aware of her heartbeat; the tiny squeaks from under the metaphoric 'ocean of . . . leaves'; the ambient hum of summer. She's peaceful but alert, and with heightened senses. I imagine her closing her eyes before the thought comes to her . . . *I am the only one.*

So, how to liberate children? How to get them to 'go for it', to relax them into believing that they can't get it wrong? How to encourage them to write free verse?

Stage 1

Read them lots of examples of free verse (see Further Reading).

Stage 2

Introduce them to the concept of a 'found' poem.

Found poems

This is a legitimate and fun way of creating poems (see also *A Poetry Teacher's Toolkit* Book 2, Ch. 1). It is a piece of writing, not poetry, that can be presented as a poem with a bit of manipulation.

The following text is taken from two newspapers, one a tabloid and the other a broadsheet.

From the tabloid:

Three baby doves
were saved from
starvation
after bird lover Mary Frink,
63, of Suffolk,
let them eat food

out of her mouth.

And from the broadsheet:

The bullet
from a 9mm weapon
was embedded
in an upstairs window frame.

They are copied word for word but are set out as free verse. The second is distinctly haiku-like, but some people would belittle it as nothing more than prose posing as poetry. Frankly, I don't **give** a hoot. If they don't want to accept it as poetry, they can give it any darn name they like.

But for me, there **are** added dimensions by laying these pieces out in this way.

- We pay more attention to the words because of their isolation in a white space.
- Line breaks, which may be thought of as a different kind of punctuation, add significance by slowing down the pace of our reading, thereby constantly making us readjust our focus.

Look at it from another point a view. Here's a piece of 'prose' by Ted Hughes:

'Only the sound of the sea, chewing away at the edge of the rocky beach, where the bits and pieces of the Iron Man lay scattered far and wide, silent and unmoving.' (From *The Iron Man*, Faber and Faber, 1968.)

- It's poetry.
- Put line breaks after 'sea' and 'edge', and the first 14 syllables are even in perfect meter (dactyl).
- It isn't a 'proper' sentence, according to the rules of prose.
- Ted Hughes couldn't have hidden the fact that he was a poet even if he tried.

So, we have the concept of the prose poem. And if we can have poetry written as prose, I rest my case. Anyway, back to 'found' poems for:

Stage 3

Select the 'best bits' from the chosen piece of writing.
From the same broadsheet, undoctored:

'A lock of brown hair and a note headed "Anne", recording the child's illness and place of burial, were carefully placed inside the box, which is covered in morocco leather, alongside envelopes and pens. A leaf torn from a notebook displays a map of a churchyard and the words "Annie Darwin's grave at Malvern".'

Now imagine you had never read that particular clip.

A lock of brown hair
and a note headed 'Anne'
recording the child's illness
are carefully laid inside a box.

A leaf torn from a notebook
displays the map of a churchyard.

It works for me. Try it out on a colleague before showing them the original. Would it be improved by adding a title?

From the same paper again:

> The jade-encrusted tomb
> of a Maya king
> has been unearthed
> in Honduras.
>
> The remains of
> a two-year-old child,
> painted red,
> and a noblewoman
> were beside the monarch.
>
> Both were sacrificed
> in honour
> of the king.

I believe that this has more impact and, in a very real sense, more meaning than the original reportage. The original piece was much longer but, by stopping where I have, I have given greater emphasis to the eight words that hit me hardest. It **is** poetry, so there!

 ## WRITING ACTIVITY: Looking for 'found' poems

Before getting children to try this, bring in several clippings and do a whole-class session at the board discussing options for pruning, word substitution and layout.

Investigate sources other than newspapers, such as fact books from the school library. I had one particularly nasty 'poem' published on the procedure for making an Egyptian mummy – kids love it! Get the children to see if they can 'find' any poems in pieces of prose that they have already written.

*   Stress to them that some words are more important than others, e.g. 'Get children find poems in prose they written' (I'm not holding that up as a good example of writing, just making the point).
*   Rule of thumb: if the poem won't 'miss' a particular word, leave it out.
*   Their experience of writing concisely to create haiku should help here.
*   Line breaks are crucial in 'free' and 'found' verse, so get the children to experiment with different layouts (much easier on the computer, of course).

Brownie points for this activity:

- Children don't have to think up the words.
- Presented as a challenge, they love to find a 'hidden' poem.
- It makes them read carefully.
- They can experiment without risk.
- Get them to read their poems out loud, deciding whether there should be any kind of pause (caesura) at the end of each line.

Stage 4

Hopefully, with the experience of the previous three stages, children will now have more confidence to write their own free verse from scratch.

- Remind them that it's only **regular** rhythm and rhyme that are being ignored.
- They can still use other devices in the poet's toolkit: simile, metaphor, personification, anthropomorphism, alliteration, assonance, internal rhyme.
- Any words that the poem won't miss should be edited out.

'If a poet writes entirely in metaphor, using rare words only, the result is jargon. But, he who uses merely commonplace words sacrifices all to clarity.' (Aristotle)

THE LITERACY HOUR: YEARS 3 AND 4

National Literacy Strategy objectives: Years 3 and 4

Year 3
- To distinguish between rhyming/non-rhyming poetry; comment on impact of layout.
- To take account of grammar and punctuation . . . when reading aloud.
- To continue the collection of new words from reading . . . and make use of them in reading and writing.

Year 4
- To compare poetic phrasing with narrative/descriptive examples.
- To practise using commas to mark grammatical boundaries within sentences and to link to work on editing and revising own writing.
- To use alternative words/expressions which are more . . . interesting than common choices.

Chosen poem

Earth Apples by Gerard Benson (p. 76)

Materials needed

Flipchart or board/marker pens
'Non-poem' version of the chosen poem (see 'Preparation')
Enlarged copy of the chosen poem (see 'Preparation')
Activity sheets and stimulus cards (see 'Preparation')
Pens, pencils, writing paper/books
Dictionaries and thesauruses
Anthologies of poetry that contain some examples of free verse
Group 4's writing books
Old newspapers (preferably tabloid)

Preparation

Type the poem on a computer, then print it out, as follows:

> 'When I read in my old book that in this island, long ago, they ate cucumbers, calling them earth-apples, I don't know why, but my heart jumped for joy. Now

with my summer meals I eat apples of the earth in cool round slices, and share the Garden of Eden with a poet who lived one thousand years ago.'

Enlarge this for the whole-class session, or write it by hand on the flipchart.

Make an enlarged copy of the chosen poem and cover it.

Make a set of stimulus cards with an idea for a poem written on each. For example, *My favourite food*, *When the hamster went missing*, *The football team was trounced*, *The trick I played on Aunty Flo*, etc. Make enough for each child in Group 1 plus three or four more.

Make copies of the activity sheets for each child, according to achievement level (photocopiable sheets 2a, 2b, 2c on pp. 65–67).

With the whole class

- Ask the children whether anyone knows what 'Earth apples' are. If they don't know, ask them to guess and jot their ideas on the board. Leave them up to look at later.
- Show the children the page with *Earth Apples* written as a piece of prose and ask a volunteer to read it. Look at the ideas for 'Earth apples' written at the beginning of the session. Did anyone guess correctly?
- Ask the children where they think the piece of writing may have come from – for example, a magazine or a newspaper. Ask them to tell you why they think this.
- Explain that the piece is actually a poem. Uncover the 'correct' version and share it with the children letting them follow the text as you read.
- When you have finished, discuss how it is different from the 'prose' version. For example, its format is now in two verses, the sentences are broken up into the lines of the verses, some words have capital letters which are not in the prose version.
- Does the poem format make a difference to the way the children perceive the mood of the piece? Ask them to tell you why or why not. Are there rhymes in the poem? Is there a pattern to it? Is it still a poem? Which version is more interesting? Why? Which version do the children prefer? Why?
- Explain that poems such as *Earth Apples* are called 'free verse'. Can anyone suggest why? Remind the children that free verse doesn't have a regular rhythm, but it can still have other features of poetry such as metaphor and simile, alliteration and assonance, personification, imagery or rhyme.
- Ask volunteers to tell you what these mean. Can they give you examples as well?
- Focus on *Earth Apples* and look for any of these features. For example, 'earth-apples' is an example of a kenning; 'my heart jumped for joy' is personification; there's assonance in 'I', 'island' and 'why', 'Now', 'round' and 'thousand'.
- Write a class poem together as free verse. Brainstorm ideas using a class experience as the basis, e.g. a trip out, a school play or performance or something funny that happened in a lesson. Agree several sentences and then work together to put them into the poem format. At this stage, don't push for any poetic features such as alliteration or metaphor and simile, although if the children come up with some, all the better. Experiment with layout, line breaks, word deletion and how it sounds when read aloud.

- Leave the final version on the board or flipchart and leave it up for the children to refer to later.
- Tell them they're going to do some more work on free verse in their groups.

Group and independent work (differentiated groups)

Group 1

Give the children the stimulus cards, their writing books and some dictionaries and thesauruses. Let them work in pairs or groups of three. They should choose a card and then write a poem in free verse about the subject written on the card. Remind them that their poem doesn't need a regular rhythm and it doesn't have to rhyme. Encourage them to begin by writing some sentences about the subject and then playing around with the layout. They should draft and redraft until they are satisfied with their work before writing the final version on a separate sheet of paper.

Group 2

Give the group the anthologies of poetry. Ask the children to explore them for examples of free verse and choose one or two favourites to share at the plenary session.

Group 3

Give out the activity sheets 2a (for lower achievers), 2b (for average achievers) and 2c (for higher achievers) and ask the children to complete them.

Group 4

Give the children in the group their writing books and ask them to choose a piece of work they did previously. They should select a portion of this (a few sentences, according to achievement level) and set it out as a poem, in free verse form. Let them look at *Earth Apples* for support and to jog their memories. Remind them they can play around with their sentences in any way they wish until they are happy with their work. They should write the final version on a separate sheet of paper.

Group 5

Give the newspapers to the group and ask them to work in pairs. They should choose a short article and work together to write it as a 'found' poem (see activity above, p. 57). Remind them that the layout will help to make the article into a poem form.

Plenary session (whole class)

- Challenge the class to tell you what free verse is. Ask the children from Group 2 to share with the class their favourite free verse poem. Why did they choose their poems?
- Did the children who wrote poems find the task difficult? Why or why not? What would they do on a second attempt to improve their work?
- Share *Earth Apples* once more, encouraging the children to join in as you read.

THE LITERACY HOUR: YEARS 5 AND 6

National Literacy Strategy objectives: Years 5 and 6

Year 5

- To understand terms which describe different kinds of poems [specifically 'free verse'] and to identify typical features.
- To understand the basic conventions of standard English.
- To apply knowledge of spelling rules and to transform words.

Year 6

- To recognise how poets manipulate words.
- To revise from Year 5 the conventions of standard English.
- To experiment with language.

Chosen poem

Propper English by Alan F. G. Lewis (p. 71)

Materials needed

Flipchart or board
Marker pens
Enlarged copy of the chosen poem (see 'Preparation')
Enlarged newspaper cutting (see 'Preparation')
The same cutting put into a free verse format (see 'Preparation')
Copies of the same cutting for Group 3
Activity sheets (see 'Preparation')
Copies of the chosen poem for each child in Group 2 (see 'Preparation')
Glue, sugar paper, scissors
Pens, pencils, writing paper/books
Dictionaries and thesauruses
Old newspapers and magazines

Preparation

Enlarge the chosen poem and make a copy.

Choose a short piece from a newspaper and enlarge it on the photocopier. Make the piece into a free verse poem and write it on the flipchart or board (see section above, p. 57). Cover it up. Make enough copies of the cutting for each child in Group 3.

Type the chosen poem using a 20-point font on a computer and print a copy for each child in Group 2.

Make copies of the activity sheets for each child, according to achievement level (photocopiable sheets 2aa, 2bb, 2cc on pp. 68–70). Give the group some old magazines or newspapers.

With the whole class

(NB: It is important that the children can see the text of this poem while you are reading it to them.)

- Show the title of the poem to the children and ask whether they notice anything. Can they suggest why 'propper' is spelt like this? Invite someone to tell you the correct spelling and ask them to check it in the dictionary. Can the children guess what this poem is about?
- Share the poem, letting the children follow the text while you read. (Make sure you read '. . . of out order', not '. . . out of order' in line four!) Did the children enjoy the poem? Encourage them to say why or why not. Do they think it's funny? Why or why not?
- Spend some time exploring the poem, teasing out what is amusing about each line. Can the children tell you what the 'correct' version of each line is? Are there any words they don't understand? For example, 'exaggerate', 'clichés' or 'infinitives'. Ask different children to check the unfamiliar words in a dictionary.
- Can anyone tell you whether the poem has a rhyme pattern? Does it have a regular rhythm? Is it a poem? Explain that it is indeed a poem but we call it 'free verse'. Do any of the children know what free verse is? Point out that free verse doesn't have a regular rhythm, but it can still have other features of poetry such as metaphor and simile, alliteration and assonance, personification, imagery or rhyme.
- Ask volunteers to tell you what each of these means. Can they give you examples as well? Are there any of these features in the chosen poem? For example, alliteration in 'sometimes split' or 'forget to finish'.
- Read the enlarged copy of the newspaper cutting to the children. Tell them that this can be used for free verse and explain that you have done this. Share the poem you made from the cutting before telling them that this is known as a 'found poem'. Invite the children to experiment with the original cutting to make another poem. Their line breaks and verse form may be totally different from yours, but this is perfectly acceptable. Let the children guide you as to the final form they want the poem to take. Write it on the flipchart and leave it up for the group session.

Group and independent work (differentiated groups)

Group 1

Give out copies of the activity sheets 2aa (for lower achievers), 2bb (for average achievers) and 2cc (for higher achievers) and ask the children to complete them.

Group 2

Give the children copies of *Propper English*, the glue, the sugar paper and the scissors. Ask them to cut the poem into its individual lines and then make another poem by putting them into a different order. Remind them that their poem must make sense, but it will still be free verse. When they are satisfied with their new poem, they should stick it onto the sugar paper. Make a display with the new poems.

Group 3

Give the children copies of the newspaper cutting used during the whole-class session. Ask them to make a poem from it, letting them look at the class version for support, although they should make up their own poem. They could work in pairs for this activity.

Group 4

Give the group an old newspaper or magazine and ask the children to choose part of a short article. They should work together to make their extract into a poem (see activity above, p. 57). Let them look at the found poem written during the whole-class session for support. Encourage them to experiment with layout and line breaks until they agree their final version.

Plenary session (whole class)

- Does everyone know what 'free verse' is? Do all the children understand what a 'found poem' is? Ask someone to tell you what each of these terms means.
- Do the children prefer writing free verse and/or found poems to more traditional poetry? Why or why not? Which do they find easier? Why?
- Share *Propper English* again, asking a volunteer to read it. Remind them to be careful in line four!

SHEET 2a

Name _____

Delete the wrong words in these sentences about free verse. One has been done for you.

Free verse is poetry / ~~cheap~~.

It does / does not have a regular rhythm.

It can still have a regular rhythm / rhyme.

Sometimes it has alliteration / a regular rhythm.

Complete these sentences. You could use the words at the bottom to help you.

Jack rushed home to see his _____. When he got there, he found _____. He was very _____. For the rest of the day he _____.

dog   six puppies   happy   played with them

gorilla   four gorillas   surprised   swung in the trees in his garden

Now put them into a free verse form. Don't forget to give your poem a title.

_____

_____

_____

_____

_____

_____

SHEET 2b

Name _____

Delete the wrong words in these sentences about free verse. One has been done for you.

Free verse is poetry / ~~cheap~~.

It does not / does have a regular rhythm.

It can still have rhyme / a regular rhythm.

Sometimes it has a regular rhythm / metaphors.

Free verse can have a regular beat / similes, too.

Complete these sentences.

Lucy was _____ when she spotted the monster. Very slowly she _____. Suddenly it turned and _____. In terror, Lucy _____.

Now put them into a free verse form. Don't forget to give your poem a title.

_____

_____

_____

_____

_____

_____

_____

_____

SHEET 2c

Name _____

Delete the wrong words in these sentences about free verse. One has been done for you.

> Free verse is poetry / ~~cheap~~.
> It does not / does have a regular rhythm.
> It can still have a regular rhythm / rhymes.
> Sometimes it has a regular rhythm / alliteration.
> Free verse can have a regular beat / similes as well.
> It might include metaphors / a rhythmic pattern.

Write a few sentences about one of these subjects:

The Frightened Ghost   How Mum Lost Me   I Played in the World Cup

(You don't have to write on all the lines, but you should write at least four sentences.)

_____

_____

_____

_____

_____

_____

Now put them into a free verse form. Don't forget to give your poem a title.

_____

_____

_____

_____

_____

SHEET 2aa

Name _____

Choose the right answer to complete these sentences about free verse and found verse.

Free verse is _____ (poetry; songs)

It does not have _____ (a regular rhythm; rhymes)

Found verse can come from _____ (newspaper articles; poetry with a regular rhythm)

We can write it from _____ (our other writing; magazine stories)

Find a short article in a magazine and stick it here.

Now write it as a found poem:

SHEET 2bb

Name _____

Choose the right answer to complete these sentences about free verse and found verse.

Free verse is _____ (poetry; songs)

It does not have _____ (a regular rhythm; rhymes)

It can still have _____ (rhymes; a regular beat)

Sometimes it has _____ (metaphors; a regular rhythm)

Free verse can have _____ (a regular beat; similes, too)

Found verse can come from _____ (newspaper articles; poetry with a regular rhythm)

We can write it from _____ (our other writing; magazine stories)

Find a short article in a magazine and stick it here.

Now write it as a found poem:

SHEET 2cc

Name _____

Choose the right answer to complete these sentences about free verse and found verse.

Free verse is _____ (poetry; prose)

It does not have _____ (rhymes; a regular rhythm)

Sometimes it has _____ (a regular rhythm; assonance)

It can have _____ (a regular rhythm; personification)

Free verse can have _____ (a regular beat; similes, too)

Found verse can come from _____ (poetry with a regular rhythm; magazines)

We can also write it from _____ (newspapers; paintings)

Find a short article in a magazine and stick it here.

Now write it as a found poem:

Propper English

Alan F. G. Lewis

Once upon a time I used
To mispell
To sometimes split infinitives
To get words of out order
To punctuate, badly
To confused my tenses
to ignore my capitals
To employ 'common or garden' clichés
To exaggerate hundreds of times a day
But worst of all I used
To forget to finish what I

In the Wood

Sheila Simmons

One, two, three, four,
They've begun to count . . .
I race into the wood to hide
Thump down the dry-mud track
Dive off through grass and hazel clumps
Crash between bracken-stalks and snatching
brambles
Crouch in a secret hollow.
Wait.

Echoing 'Cooeee's'
As they follow;
Laughter,
Crack of branches
As they call my name,
Call; call again,
Then stop.

Foxgloves rear up all around me
Dragon-necked, with purple tongues;
Fern-fronds lay long hands over me
Stifling with the greenness of their heavy smell;
Swarms of small flies annoy.

The wood falls quiet;
I hear my heart;
Then some minute wild squeaking
Deep in the ocean of the leaves.
Upon the air a thin dynamic hum,
The sound of summer.
No other person in the world but me.

The Dismantled Ship

Walt Whitman

In some unused lagoon, some nameless bay,
On sluggish, lonesome waters, anchor'd near the shore,
An old, dismasted, grey and batter'd ship, disabled, done,
After free voyages to all the seas of earth, haul'd up at last and
  hawser'd tight,
Lies rusting, mouldering.

The Ship Starting

Walt Whitman

Lo, the unbounded sea,
On its breast a ship starting, spreading all sails, carrying even her
  moonsails.
The pennant is flying aloft as she speeds she speeds so stately –
below emulous waves press forward,
They surround the ship with shining curving motions and foam.

Vesuvius

Mike and Nicky Jubb

Smouldering smoke stack;
restless, unreasoning,
simmering, seething, volatile volcano;
a deep, dangerous furnace.

Earth's chimney slumbers
like a dormant dragon.
But its belly grumbles
and the ground trembles
to the echo of its rumbling.

It starts awake,
quaking the earth
making mischief
in hot-headed eruption.

No time for conscience or corruption;
no time to say their prayers,
or 'goodbye'. The merciless mountain
explodes in savage temper
and rains instant death,

vomiting volcanic ash
and oozing molten lava.

Overpowering
devouring element;

making statues out of real people.

Two Sisters

Mike Jubb

I was on my own, doing what I like doing best,
being on my own.

Wandering through the churchyard of a quiet, one street village,
the headstones told me just a little of the lives and loves
and deaths of the folk that were buried there.

This one was special:

IN
LOVING MEMORY OF
DEAR LITTLE PATSY
INFANT DAUGHTER OF
JACK AND ELSA BEDE
DIED APRIL 25TH 1892
AGED 15 MONTHS

ALSO HER SISTER
KATHLENE ANNE BEDE
DIED FEBRUARY 4TH 1989
AGED 93 YEARS

Two sisters, who never knew each other, are buried together:
one whose life had only just started,
and one who lived to be very old.

They died 97 years apart.
Patsy, who was born first, will always be a baby.
Kathlene Anne, the younger sister who never married,
will be remembered only
as an old lady.

Earth Apples

Gerard Benson

When I read in my old book
That in this island, long ago,
They ate cucumbers,
Calling them earth-apples,
I don't know why,
But my heart jumped for joy.

Now with my summer meals
I eat apples of the earth
In cool round slices,
And share the Garden of Eden
With a poet who lived
One thousand years ago.

Midnight Meeting

Mike Jubb

On soft, silent, padded paws,
all cats are grey in the night;
this is their time.

A shadow walking in shadows,
Prometheus is on the prowl.
Other toms keep their distance,
and a fox crosses the road
to avoid him;
but the mouse saw nothing,
heard nothing,
knew nothing.

On wings without a whisper,
old Tawny perches
on the chimney pot
in time to see the cat
snatch his prey.
Their eyes meet,
the owl and the pussycat,
the staring match of all time.

Prometheus looks away first.
After all,
he has the mouse.

3 You'd Better Shape Up!

Featured poems

A Long and Sad Tale by Lewis Carroll
Where Can It Be? by Mike Jubb
Call That Music? by Paul Bright
Rhino by Gina Douthwaite
Shadow by Gina Douthwaite
Kite by Mike Jubb
I Wonder If the Moon by Andrea Marsh

'Concrete poetry is a form of cementics created by mortar bards.' (David Orme)
(That well-known anagram, 'I'm odd Vera'.)

Shape poetry

Shape poetry is the general term used when the layout of the words reflects the theme of the poem in some way; 'concrete' poetry and calligrams can be viewed as sub-sections. Both are a kind of word sculpture, but with calligrams the actual typography and shape of the letters is involved. Calligrams that have no poetic content, such as

SLIMLINE

are merely graphics in my view.

George Herbert wrote a shape poem on a religious theme in the seventeenth century but, with exceptions like Lewis Carroll's classic, *A Long and Sad Tale* (p. 100), it's only in recent years that this device has become popular with writers and publishers of children's poetry. Now, there are many published examples that you can show to children (see Further Reading).

'Show' being the important word, of course, because shape poetry is the one type of poetry that tends to lack impact when it's read aloud. So, when you want your kids to have a go, it might be an idea to photocopy as many as you can and make a display of them first, just to open up their minds to the possibilities.

I haven't written many shape poems myself – I can't draw with a pencil, let alone with words – so I sympathise deeply with any child who finds it difficult.

WRITING ACTIVITY: Starting with shapes

An easy way to make a start is to draw a **faint** outline and fill it with a collection of words about the subject, e.g. a leaf, for words about autumn. You may already have done something like this after brainstorming words for a topic (for more on brainstorming see Chapter 4).

Let the children use a template if necessary, to ensure that the inside space is adequate for the job. Start by using uncomplicated shapes, with the children writing from left to right, and from top to bottom, as normal. And encourage them to work from, and to, the edges of the shape. When it's full, the outline can be erased, leaving the basic shape behind. Extra details can always be drawn in, such as the stalk of a leaf, to help with the illusion.

Small gaps should be left between words, of course, but it might be an idea to have adjacent words in different colours, just to help readability. Get them to experiment. **Alternatively**, words can be written around the outside of a shape.

The writing of my poem *Where Can It Be?* (p. 101) was very much a matter of coming up with an idea and then experimenting until I found a combination of words that satisfied me. Trial and error (also known as 'suck it and see') writing is more creative than some mysterious divine inspiration. I'm forever trying to get children to see that **playing around with words makes things happen**. I'm far from being the only poet to use the isosceles triangle as the basis for a shape poem, so there's no reason why your children shouldn't use it again for: a magician's hat, a witch's hat, a pyramid, a funnel (base over apex), or just words about triangles.

This shape also lends itself very nicely to being composed on the computer. All you have to do is select the 'centre text' option, and what you see is what you get. Fitting a word into the pointy top of the triangle is a problem; it cries out for a capital 'A', which means the kids will have to start stringing words together.

WRITING ACTIVITY: First shape poems

Once children have made a few attempts at creating shapes out of word collections, encourage them to use those same shapes again, but this time with more 'meaning' rather than simply a collection of words. They don't have to worry about it being a 'poem'. My poem *Where Can It Be?* is a rather unimpressive piece of prose when you read it out loud – it's the interaction between the words and the shape that counts.

Shape monsters

Use a straight-sided geometric shape for the body: square, rhombus, diamond, rectangles, parallelograms and trapeziums of varying proportions. The title could be *The Rectangular Monster* etc. Once the body has been filled and the outline erased, the rest can be drawn in: arms, legs, tentacles, heads, horns, tails, etc.

Shape robots: *similar idea*

Rhino by Gina Douthwaite (p. 103)

This splendid and sophisticated shape poem shows what can be achieved with experience, a talented feel for words and a lot of hard work. Less commonly for a shape poem, this one **is** successful when read aloud. Its strict meter and rhyme enable it to stand alone perfectly well without the shape element.

> When more than one rhinoceros becomes rhinoceroses,
> and each of these has horns of hair that stick up from their noses,
> and armoured skin that wallows in the mud when they reposes,
> and on each foot each rhino has three hooves instead of toeses –
> the features of these creatures show the problem language poses
> when more than one rhinoceros becomes rhinoceroses.

Can't you just hear that being sung to Sullivan's music? The main wordplay here is obviously the mispronunciation of 'rhinoceroses' so that it rhymes with 'noses', and the false plural 'toeses'. But it is also worth pointing out to the children how the modest use of alliteration ('has horns of hair'), and the internal rhyme of 'features' and 'creatures', add to the musicality of a very rhythmic piece.

However, Gina's clever marrying up of words with shape adds a whole new dimension to the poem. But it's got to be worth letting your children see and hear the 'straight' version first before hitting them with the real thing – the impact will be greater and it'll impress the socks off them.

*   *   *

Rhino really is a good poem to use with the kids. It's also a super way of stimulating them to make their own shape poems based on animals: giraffes, rabbits, snakes, frogs, etc. – the possibilities are endless and the children love to do it!

Shape poems are among my favourites – there are some very clever and very amusing examples doing the rounds. Ask the kids to keep an eye out for some and encourage them to make a class anthology. Everyone could include their particular favourite. [C.D.]

THE LITERACY HOUR: YEARS 3 AND 4

National Literacy Strategy objectives: Years 3 and 4

Year 3
- To . . . comment on the impact of layout.
- To notice and investigate a range of other devices for presenting texts.
- To use word banks and dictionaries.

Year 4
- To write poems experimenting with different styles and structures.
- To reread own writing to check for grammatical sense.
- To use word banks and dictionaries.

Chosen poem

Kite by Mike Jubb (p. 105)

Materials needed

Enlarged copy of the chosen poem
Flipchart or board
Marker pens
Enlarged copy of calligram words (photocopiable sheet on p. 87)
Copies of the same sheet for Group 2
Pens, pencils, writing paper/books
Selection of templates – a variety of animal shapes, fruit and vegetable shapes and geometric shapes
Activity sheets (see 'Preparation')
Dictionaries and thesauruses

Preparation

Enlarge the chosen poem and the photocopiable sheet on p. 87.
    Make copies of the photocopiable sheet for each child in Group 2.
    Make copies of the activity sheets for each child, according to achievement level (photocopiable sheets 3a, 3b, 3c on pp. 88–90 and shape sheets a, b and c on pp. 89, 91, 93).

With the whole class

- Before sharing *Kite*, show it to the children and discuss the shape of the text. Can they tell you what the poem might be about? Why do they think this? Does anyone know the general term for poems presented like this? Explain that they are called **shape poems**.

- Share *Kite* with the children letting them follow the text as you read. Did they guess correctly what the poem is about? Why do they think the text is written in this particular way? Does it help them to imagine the kite more easily?

- Ask the children what makes this poem different from others they have explored and whether they like this form of poetry. Encourage them to tell you why or why not.

- Spend some time exploring the poem in more detail. What are the rhymes in the poem? ('my/high/eye'; 'moon/soon') Is there any alliteration? ('hopes are high', 'my mind's . . .', 'my/moon') Can the children give you an example of assonance? (Much of the top half of the kite shape has examples.) Why does the poet use so many words with the phoneme 'ie'? (Perhaps to continually echo the word 'high', giving an image of the kite constantly straining ever higher to reach the moon.) How do the children react to following the kite-tail down when they read to the end of the poem? Do they think the poet still feels hopeful and 'on a high'? Why or why not? Do they like the poem? Why or why not? Do they think it was a good idea to write it in the shape of a kite? Would it have had the same impact if presented more traditionally? Why or why not?

- What other objects would make a good shape poem? For example, a triangle, an apple or a fish. List the children's suggestions on the board and leave them up. Choose one of the templates and brainstorm some words that are associated with it – write these on the board and leave them up.

- Explain to the children that the two main types of shape poems are **concrete poems** and **calligrams**. Does anyone know the difference? (Year 4 children should remember this from their work in Year 3.) Point out that the text of a concrete poem is usually set out in a way that reflects the subject of the poem. Explain that in a calligram, the formation of the letters or font, also does this. For example, jagged letters could be used in a poem about something frightening.

- What type of poem is *Kite*? (concrete) – challenge the children to tell you why. Write 'concrete poem' and 'calligram' on the board and leave them up while working on this lesson.

- Look at the examples of calligram words on the enlarged photocopied sheet and discuss how the font or letters help to put across the meaning of each of the words. Ask the children to suggest other things that might make good calligrams. Let them come to the board and try writing their words in a style that puts across their ideas.

- Tell the children they are going to do some more work on this in their groups.

Group and independent work (differentiated groups)

Group 1

Working closely with the children, help them to write their own poem about a kite, or alternatively, a hot air balloon. They could draw the outline in pencil first, to keep their text within shape, and rub it out when they have written the final version. Remind them their poem doesn't have to rhyme and encourage them to use dictionaries and thesauruses. Let them revise and redraft until they are satisfied with their work.

Group 2

Give each child a copy of the sheet with calligram words together with a thesaurus. Ask them to use the thesaurus to find an alternative for each word on the sheet and then write their new word as a calligram. Challenge them to invent a different 'font' from the original word on the sheet. Alternatively, they could write antonyms for some of the words on the sheet, as calligrams.

Group 3

Let the children choose one or two templates (according to achievement level) and draw around it. They should then write inside the shape words associated with it (see activity above, p. 79). For example, if they chose a dog, they could write 'bark', 'stroke', 'bone', 'greedy', 'wag', 'chase', 'sniff', 'drool', etc. Tell the children that in this way they will be making a word bank to use later for writing poetry. (At a later session, help them to put their words into a meaningful poem within the outline of the shape.)

Group 4

Give out copies of activity sheets 3a and shape sheet a (for lower achievers), 3b and shape sheet b (for average achievers) and 3c and shape sheet c (for higher achievers). Ask them to complete their sheets using dictionaries for support.

Plenary session (whole class)

- Ask for a volunteer to read the words 'calligram' and 'concrete poem'. Challenge the children to tell you what they mean.
- Read one or two of the children's calligrams and shape poems. Did they find it easy or difficult to write these? Encourage them to tell you why. Is there anything they could do to improve their work? What?
- Do the children prefer shape poems to conventional poems? Why or why not? Do they prefer concrete poems or calligrams? Why?

THE LITERACY HOUR: YEARS 5 AND 6

National Literacy Strategy objectives: Years 5 and 6

Year 5
- To use the structures of poems read to write extensions based on these . . . by substituting own ideas.
- To discuss, proofread and edit their own writing for clarity and correctness.
- To use dictionaries.

Year 6
- To articulate personal responses to literature, identifying how and why a text affects a reader.
- To form complex sentences.
- To use dictionaries and IT spell checks.

Chosen poem

Call That Music? by Paul Bright (p. 102)

Materials needed

Enlarged copy of the chosen poem
Flipchart or board
Marker pens
Enlarged copy of calligram words (photocopiable sheet on p. 87)
Copies of the same sheet for Group 1
Pens, pencils, writing paper/books
Selection of templates – a variety of animal shapes, fruit and vegetable shapes and geometric shapes
Activity sheets (see 'Preparation')
Dictionaries and thesauruses
Word cards (see 'Preparation')
A3 paper (or equivalent).

Preparation

Enlarge the chosen poem but cover the title.

Enlarge the chosen poem and the photocopiable sheet on p. 87.

Make copies of the photocopiable sheet for each child in Group 1.

Make copies of the activity sheets for each child, according to achievement level (photocopiable sheets 3aa, 3bb, 3cc on pp. 91–93 and shape sheets aa, bb and cc on pp. 89–93).

Prepare a set of cards, each with a stimulus word written on it that lends itself to being a calligram. For example, 'cold', 'laugh', 'jump', 'stretch', 'low', 'gate', 'curly', etc.

With the whole class

- Before sharing *Call That Music?* show it to the children (but don't read it yet) and discuss the shape that the text is written in. Can they tell you what the poem might be about? Why do they think this? Uncover the title and ask for more guesses. Is the shape now just a circle or does it represent something else? (a CD) Does anyone know the general term for poems presented like this? Explain that they are called **shape poems**.

- Starting at the line 'Call that music?' share the poem with the children, letting them follow the text as you read. Did they like the poem? Why or why not? Has anyone had a similar experience at home with their own music or a sibling's? Ask a volunteer to tell the class about it.

- Ask the children what makes this poem different from others they have explored and whether they like shape poems. Encourage them to tell you why or why not.

- Spend some time exploring the poem in more detail. What do the children notice about the end/beginning of the poem? Do they think this 'never-ending' device is clever? Is there a verse pattern to the poem as it stands? If the poem was written in a traditional way, what regular verse patterns could there be? (For example, four verses of four lines, two verses of eight lines, or one verse of 16 lines.) Is there a rhyme pattern? (ABCB) Is it possible to start anywhere in the poem and still make sense of it? Do the children like the idea of putting a poem about music inside the shape of a CD? Why or why not?

- What other objects would make a good shape poem? For example, a telephone, a snake or a boomerang. List the children's suggestions on the board and leave them up. Choose one of the templates and brainstorm some words that are associated with it – write these on the board and leave them up.

- Explain to the children that the two main types of shape poems are **concrete poems** and **calligrams**. Does anyone know the difference? Remind the children that the text of a concrete poem is usually set out in a way that reflects the subject of the poem. Explain that in a calligram, the formation of the letters or font also does this. For example, 'shivering' letters could be used in a poem about ice and snow.

- What type of poem is *Call That Music?* (concrete) – challenge the children to tell you why. Write 'concrete poem' and 'calligram' on the board and leave them up while working on this lesson.

- Look at the examples of calligram words on the enlarged photocopied sheet and discuss how the font or letters help to put across the meaning of each of the words. Ask the children to suggest other things that might make good calligrams. Let them come to the board and try writing their words in a style that puts across their ideas.

- Tell the children they are going to do some more work on this in their groups.

Group and independent work (differentiated groups)

Group 1

Give each child a copy of the sheet with calligram words together with a dictionary and thesaurus. Ask them to find an antonym for each word on the sheet and then write their new word as a calligram.

Group 2

Give out copies of activity sheets 3aa and shape sheet aa (for lower achievers), 3bb and shape sheet bb (for average achievers) and 3cc and shape sheet cc (for higher achievers). Encourage the children to use dictionaries and thesauruses for support.

Group 3

Give the children the stimulus word cards, in a pile, face down. They should turn over each card and write the word on the A3 paper in calligram form.

Group 4

Let the children work in pairs and choose a template as a subject for a shape poem and draw around it. They should then brainstorm for words associated with it, for their poem, and list them on paper (see activity above, p. 87). Using their mini word banks, they should agree a short poem that they can write in the outline of the shape. Remind them that their poem doesn't have to rhyme, and they should draft and redraft until they are happy with their work.

Plenary session (whole class)

- Ask the children to tell you what 'shape poetry', 'calligrams' and 'concrete poems' are.
- Ask one or two of the children to show their calligrams or shape poems. Did they find it easy or difficult to write these? Ask them to say why. How could they improve their work?
- Do the children prefer shape poems to conventional poems? Why or why not? Do they prefer concrete poems or calligrams? Why?

PHOTOCOPIABLE SHEET

hIGh

funny!

SKINNY

TIRED zzzzz

LONG

C-C-C-C-COLD

S-c-c-c-a-a-r-r-r-r-y . . .

OVER HARD

HEAVY

SHEET 3a

Name _____

Read *Kite* by Mike Jubb. What is shape poetry?

_____

Now look at the shape on your shape sheet and write a poem inside it. You could use some of the words below to help you. Use this space to draft your shape poem

brown	orange	tall	long	neck	legs
tongue	leaves	tail	flick	eyes	blink

SHAPE SHEET a

SHEET 3b

Name _____

Read *Kite* by Mike Jubb. What is shape poetry?

_____

What is a concrete poem?

_____

Now look at the shape on your shape sheet and write a poem inside it. You could use some of the words below to help you. Use this space to draft your shape poem.

slithering   long   shiny   tongue   flickering

sideways   grass   pattern   skin

SHAPE SHEET b

SHEET 3c

Name _____

Read *Kite* by Mike Jubb. What is shape poetry?

_____

What is a concrete poem?

_____

What is a calligram?

_____

Now look at the shape on your shape sheet and write a poem inside it. Use this space to draft your shape poem.

SHAPE SHEET c

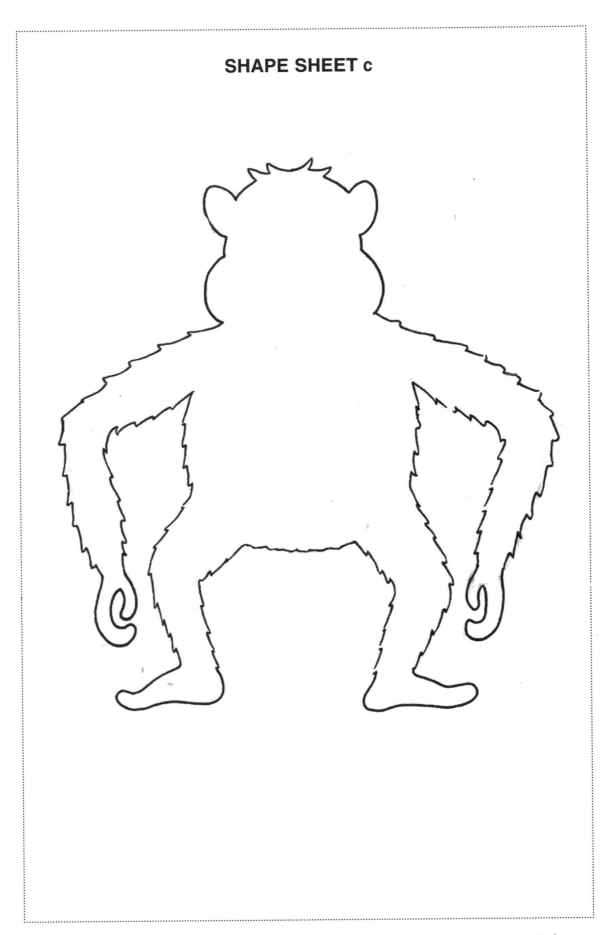

SHEET 3aa

Name _____

Read *Call That Music?* by Paul Bright. What kind of poem is it? There are some words below to help you.

_____

What is a concrete poem?

_____

What is a calligram?

_____

shape   inside   letters   form   poem   about

Now look at the shape on your shape sheet and write a poem inside it. You could use the words below to help you. Use this space to draft your space poem.

machine   metal   buttons   clanking   rusty   flashing lights   crazy

SHAPE SHEET aa

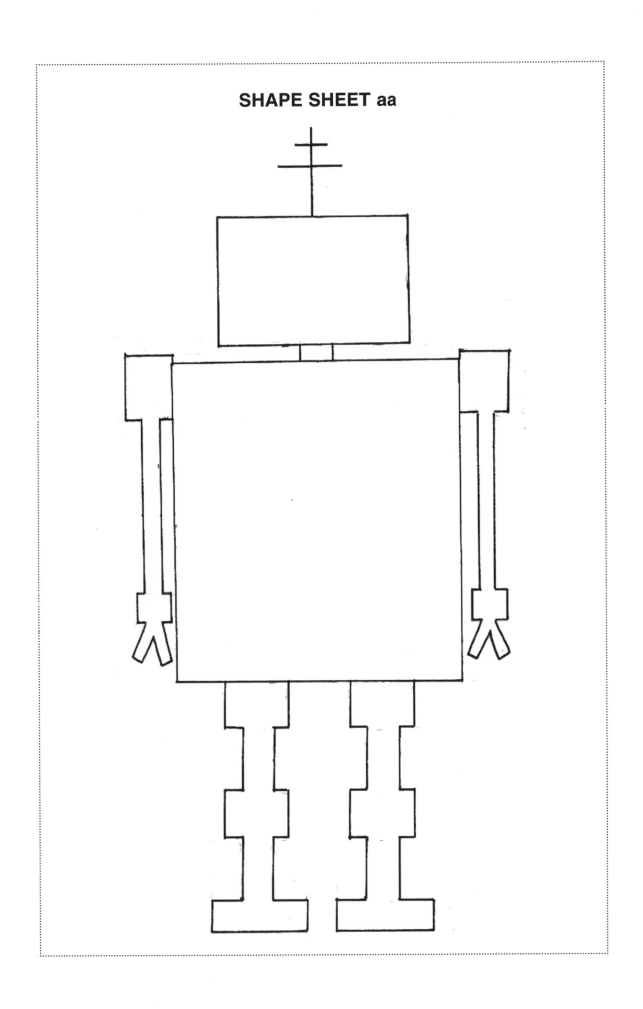

SHEET 3bb

Name _____

Read *Call That Music?* by Paul Bright. What kind of poem is it?

_____

What is a concrete poem?

_____

What is a calligram?

_____

Now look at the shape on your shape sheet and write a poem inside it. You could use the words below to help you. Use this space to draft your shape poem.

scary   friendly   huge   loud   hairy   slow   noisy

SHAPE SHEET bb

SHEET 3cc

Name _____

Read *Call That Music?* by Paul Bright. What kind of poem is it?

_____

What is a concrete poem?

_____

What is a calligram?

_____

Now look at the shape on your shape sheet and write a poem inside it. Use this space to draft your space poem.

SHAPE SHEET cc

A Long and Sad Tale

Lewis Carroll

"Fury said to
a mouse, That
he met in the
house, 'Let
us both go
to law: *I*
will prose-
cute *you.*—
Come, I'll
take no de-
nial: We
must have
the trial;
For really
this morn-
ing I've
nothing
to do.'
Said the
mouse to
the cur.
'Such a
trial, dear
Sir. With
no jury
or judge,
would
be wast-
ing our
breath.'
'I'll be
judge.
I'll be
jury,'
said
cun-
ning
old
Fury: 'I'll
try
the
whole
cause,
and
con-
demn
you to
death.'"

Where Can It Be?

Mike Jubb

A
long
time ago
there lived
a very old and
absent - minded
magician who was
always losing things,
especially his favourite hat.

Illustrated by Lisa Malhas

Call That Music?

Paul Bright

Used to play it
Night and day
Dad went crazy
And he'd say:
Call that music?
What a din!
Turn it down
Or pack it in.
What's rock music
Coming to?
Let's see what's
On Radio 2
This is music
Solid gold
Stuff like this
Just don't grow old

Rhino

Gina Douthwaite

When more than one rhinoceros becomes rhinoceroses, and each of these has horns of hair that stick up from their noses, and armoured skin that wallows in the mud when they reposes, and on each foot each rhino has three hooves instead of toeses - the features of these creatures show the problem language poses when more than one rhinoceros becomes rhinoceroses.

Shadow

Gina Douthwaite

Follows
down the footpath,
copies every stride,
creeps around the corner
when I try to hide.
Bends along the fences,
overtakes on walls -
taller, thinner,
faster,
fatter,
slower,
small.
Underneath the lamp-post
fades
as
though
it's
shy.
L-o-n-g-s
to snuggle
into   bed
when   the
moon   is
high.   Reaches
out to   touch me.
What -   ever
can it   be?
this   thing
that's   like
a twin,   this
shape   that
sticks   with me?

Kite

Mike Jubb

I
may
try to fly
my kite sky-high;
and in my mind`s eye
I too will rise delightfully into
the night-sky. My hopes are high.
I may even try to reach for the moon;
to reach for the Girl in the Moon;
delightfully reach for the Girl.
For the Girl in the Moon
is in sight. And my
hopes are as
high as a
kite.
I
M
a
y
R
e
a
c
h
F
o
r
H
e
r
S
o
o
n.
M
a
y
b
e
T
o
n
i
g
h
t

I Wonder If the Moon

Andrea Marsh (age 10)

(Redlands Primary School, Fareham – with a little help from Dad, Terry)

4 More Ways Than One

Featured poems

> *The Phoenix* by Robert Fisher
> *Roasting the Phoenix* by Jane Clarke
> *Binsey Poplars, felled 1879* by Gerard Manley Hopkins
> *The Poplar Field* by William Cowper
> *The Cuckoo Comes in April*, Anon.
> *The Cuckoo*, Anon.
> *To the Cuckoo* by William Wordsworth
> Extract from *The Kitten at Play* by William Wordsworth
> *On a Cat, Ageing* by Sir Alexander Gray
> *The Moon* by Katy Ware
> *Up in the Sky* by Rachael Oliver
> *The Moon* by Dan Fisher
> *The Bewitching Hour* by Elizabeth Bailey

Apart from new inventions and discoveries, there are no new subjects to write about. As writers, we can only try to find our own 'angle' on existing subjects, and to use words in as fresh a way as we can. This chapter offers a model for brainstorming in order to exploit different angles of the same subject.

> 'A fool is someone who doesn't know something that you've only just learned.'
> (*Reader's Digest*, circa 1383)

I've been doing some research into a business model of brainstorming.

What is brainstorming?

I suppose the definition of 'brainstorming', as it happens in most Key Stage 2 classrooms, might be something like: The class/group pooling its collective knowledge of a specific topic. At least, that was **my** understanding of 'brainstorming' until recently.
   Pooling knowledge is important, but I would like to broaden that model.

- Brainstorming can be a process for generating **new** ideas.
- Specifically, it uses certain 'rules' that encourage and spark off new thoughts **which might never have occurred otherwise**.

- When ideas merge, 2 + 2 **can** equal 5 (see the section on haiku in Chapter 1).
- Good brainstorming is thinking out loud. It gives children the chance to air all their ideas without being judged.

The main aims

- To focus the children's attention on a specific topic or problem.
- To collect **many** ideas. The more there are to choose from, the more chance of finding good'uns; it's easier to create a good'un from combining lots of little'uns.
- To teach respect for other people's ideas.
- To encourage children to take risks in sharing their thoughts.
- To demonstrate that time spent collecting 'raw materials' for writing, or problem solving, is time well spent.
- To encourage teamwork ('team thinking').

Resources

- Someone to write down all the ideas. If a classroom assistant or parent could do it, you would be free to facilitate (and not have your back turned much of the time!).
- A flipchart, or a large piece of wallpaper, is better than a board – you can then keep, and move, your results.
- Thick felt-tip pens. Different colours for adjacent ideas aids readability (and it's prettier).
- Props. Depending on the topic, it can be helpful to have some physical thing(s) in front of the children.

The scribe should:

- Write the topic in the centre of the paper.
- Keep jottings brief.
- Write the words and phrases randomly about the paper. No groupings.

For maximum success:

- All children must feel confident enough to participate. They mustn't be scared of taking creative risks.

So, what inhibits children's creativity?

- Self-censorship: fear of 'getting it wrong'.
- Self-censorship: fear of ridicule.
- Self-censorship: lack of confidence and/or self-worth.
- Boredom.
- Language problems.

So, the theory is . . .

- If children **believe** that they are creative . . . they will be!

The 'rules':
The children need to understand that:

- You want as many suggestions as possible, from **everyone**.
- It's a team effort, i.e. they are on the same side trying to inspire each other.
- Each suggestion belongs to the class, not to the child who made it.
- Every child and every idea has equal value. Therefore every idea will be welcomed and written down.
- There are no wrong answers (providing they are within the given topic).
- Little attention will be given to each suggestion at this stage (to minimise the pressure).
- No one, teacher included, is to reject or mock anyone's contribution.
- It is part of the group's job to help everyone feel they can safely contribute.
- **Actively** listening to other people's ideas might suggest something that could add/warp/exaggerate it; tell them to 'hitch hike' on their classmates' thoughts.
- You want silly, weird, bizarre suggestions, as well as the more obvious ones. A crazy remark can spark off other people.

It might be an idea to:

- Close the door and pull the blinds to minimise distractions.
- Play random selections from two CDs, one calm, one stimulating. Experiment.
- Have a 'yellow card' to show if someone is getting critical.
- Set a time limit. Experiment, but you could try ten minutes before playtime and then ten minutes after. The break might generate discussion and fresh thinking.

Method/your role:

- Create a warm, supportive atmosphere (as always!).
- Keep the session on subject.
- Praise children for joining in. Encourage and enthuse.
- Laughter at a zany thought, or an encouraging 'I like it!', is great, but negative judgement will scare off the wary.
- Evaluating ideas at this stage uses up thinking power which could be devoted to the job in hand: generating ideas. Dismiss nothing (unless it's indecent!), and gently rebuke negative responses.
- Try **not** to use children's names. You want individuals to 'melt' into the group effort.
- Work fast. You want to get them 'on a roll', to get them absorbed in the process, to think more freely. You might even need **two** scribes!
- Writers need to think fast and consider later. Speeding things up leaves less time for criticism or evaluation.

- No idea is too silly – crazy comments can stimulate new thought patterns. If children feel free to be zany, they'll stretch their minds, and new ideas are more likely to pop up.
- Be brave yourself. Risk sharing your own daft thoughts. Be a model.
- Keep telling them how well they are doing. Keep your eyes moving, making contact and smiling.
- Try to ensure that every child contributes at least one idea.

Ask questions – it can be easier to adapt an existing idea than to come up with an original one. It's a kind of second drafting.

So, use your skills in open-ended questioning.

What if . . . ?
What else could . . . ?
What can we do with . . . ?
How many ways can you . . . ?
What do you notice about . . . ?

To discourage participation:

- Pull a discouraging face.
- Ignore a child and/or their idea.
- Say 'That's wrong/not right/not what I want/not good enough', etc.
- Say 'That's a good idea, but . . . '

To encourage participation:

- Look and sound enthusiastic.
- Don't interrupt a child, or allow anyone else to.
- Say 'That's a good idea/thought/suggestion'.
- Say 'Tell me more'.
- Ask 'Can anyone add something to that?'
- Ask 'Can anyone make that into a really crazy idea?'

Troubleshooting

The child who dominates

- Try to quieten them down by gently asking them to give everyone a chance.
- Tell them that they have more ideas than you can cope with, and would they mind writing them down and giving them to you later.
- Less satisfactory – go round the class in turns asking for thoughts. You might make it a game where each child builds on the idea of the previous one.

If they start to dry up too soon

- Keep adding your own ideas – they'll soon pick up again.
- Choose one aspect of the topic already mentioned and brainstorm that separately. For example, Topic: Hedgehogs; Aspect: Nocturnal; Question: What do they do at night? Ordinary answer: They search for food. Silly answer: They go to a night-club.

After brains have been stormed

- Thank them for working so hard, and say how much you enjoyed it.
- Tell them to let you know if they get any more ideas later.

You need to decide in which form you are going to make this material available to the children. If they are going to write immediately after the brainstorm, you'll have to leave it as it is. But, if you have all been working quickly, it's bound to be a mess. Suggestions for consideration:

- Move on to something else now.
- Tell the children that you're going to sort the jumble out a bit.
- When you can, copy out ('in best') all the ideas as a straight list (unless you can volunteer a trusty helper).
- Edit out any ideas that are repeated, or too similar, but . . .
- Don't categorise or organise them in any way. Even now, random is creative.
- Display the lists as idea reservoirs, and as spelling and key vocabulary resources.
- You now have a resource that is worth keeping and can be added to whenever you like.

So I tried it out!

This is the unedited result of a Year 5/6 brainstorm on 'The Moon'.

monster	moonwalk	space
colours	blackness	magic
loony	cuckoo	romance
Neil Armstrong	Milky Way	madness
misty moonlight	aliens	phases
Michael Jackson	white	tides
moon is hollow	crazy	lunacy
loopy	holey	chunky
giant cherry	space station	werewolf
1st man	luminous	cheese
astronaut	UFO	spinning basketball
stars	lightbeam	gooey
giant football	like eating a jaffa cake	orbit

craters	asteroid	future
flower head	round	sphere
spaceship	Apollo 13	shuttle
planets	closing hammock	bumpy
galaxy	abracadabra	shimmer
star vessel	Enterprise	rubber ball
tidal waves	tulip flower with no stem	Star Prize
space chocolate	unknown creatures	satellite dish
change	moon dizzy going round	fat man (in the moon)
a giant's eye	light lasers	meteorite
skinny man (in the moon)	wake the dead	'Sailor Moon'
silver surfer	hard and lumpy	out of graves
moonlight	aurora borealis	moondust
light on water	NASA	shadows
one small step	giant's belly	rocky
flying horse	unicorn	scary wind surfer
low gravity	scrunched up paper	G force
eclipse	soft landing	night
day	silvery shivery moonbuggy	man in the moon
rapid surf	no air	4th man on the moon
giant's head	the sauce be with you (moon	is ghost of a meatball)
dark side	dust	seas on moon
crescent	half-moon	footprints
dancing in the moonlight	face	floating

Reflections on the experience

As you can see, there was no shortage of involvement, and the children were **very** industrious afterwards. I attempted to brainstorm without having 'hands up' so that the children could get their thoughts out quicker . . . well, it seemed like a good idea at the time which might have worked with a smaller number. It wasn't always easy to keep them 'on subject'. Some boys, in particular, tried to follow the UFO/alien/monster trail further than I wanted. No surprise there then.

Given a free choice, many of the children still wanted to write in rhyme, often with predictable results (see *A Poetry Teacher's Toolkit* Book 2). There are over a hundred items on the list, but the potential for thousands of poems. Some that later emerged from the session are featured on pages 107, 132, 133 and 134. These children may have had a little parental help, but that's OK. If we've involved the home, so much the better. What a great thing for kids to be sharing poetry writing with Mum or Dad. The results are pleasing and important, but it's the process that counts.

The Moon Poem (below), by Sophie Calthorpe, is something else. Sophie has clearly copied phrases directly from the brainstorm list. But she's been selective, and look at the way she's put them together. I wasn't present so I know nothing of how her thinking went . . . but I love it.

The poem has a stream of consciousness feel about it, and what a great ending.

Whether Sophie intended it or not, in my mind there is a maze of interlinking connotations: being cuckoo / lunacy; lunacy / the moon; the moon / romance; being in love / being cuckoo. As far as I'm concerned, the whole process was worthwhile just for Sophie's contribution.

The Moon Poem
by Sophie Calthorpe, age 10
(Redlands Primary School, Fareham)

The man on the moon saw a flying horse, all the stars are like a giant cherrys there are tidal waves with silver surfer, one small step and colours of crazy light beam magic shimmer, the misty moonlight looks like white milky way cheese the aliens have space chocolate and star prize Orbit, the skinny man in the moon see's the galaxy's and planets, the cuckoo's have romance every evning.

Every child wrote something and, because of the brainstorm, everyone had their own 'take' on the subject. Here are a few more phrases that appealed to me:

Katherine: 'Just the right light.'

Liam: 'I saw a fat man on the moon,
Playing a tune on a silver spoon.'

Joe: 'To him I must look like a flea.'

Zara: 'Romance spins around and around, with shadows of owls.'

Aaron: 'Today a voyage to the moon, tomorrow maybe Mars.'

Shane: 'Shadows jump from out of hollows. His cratered face looks down on me.'

Lathan: 'He must have a million lights to make him shine so bright.'

Laura: 'I walk on the moon, eat space station food.'

Hollie: 'I don't know where I'll go . . . I just saw a UFO.'

Chelsea: 'No friends to speak to, or people to see
Maybe a comet every century.'

Chay: 'The man in the moon met the girl in the sun and
Had a candlelit dinner by the light of pop stars.'

Philip: 'The sun's bright ray is cut out because of the moon.'

Esther: 'Suddenly in the blink of an eye
A cow jumped over the moon.
The monster, all his hairs on end
Tries to eat the poor old thing!'

Harry: 'Moon babies are the guarders of cheese.'

Robbie: 'Alien, alien, up in space,
What is it like in a different place?'

Rachael: 'The moon would surf around the earth
As if it did not have a care in the world.'

Callum: 'The crater was full of tomato sauce
the moon passes the sun and all the cheese
bubbles and boils and cooks the pizza for
the man on the moon who eats it.'

Michael: 'One small step for man,
One giant leap for mankind.
What will the moon be in the future?'

Collecting activity

Give the children a weekend task of finding, and copying out, a poem on a specific topic, choosing one that has many examples: cats, dogs, the wind, snow, rain, the sea, spring, summer, autumn, winter, teachers, mums, dads, grandparents, friends, siblings, witches, dragons, ghosts, Christmas.

Our featured poems for this chapter offer several pairs that approach a subject in contrasting ways. In *Binsey Poplars* (p. 131) and *The Poplar Field* (p. 132), Hopkins and Cowper both decry the felling of a favourite row of poplars. Hopkins's pain is evident in 'Not one spared, not one'; equally effective is Cowper's image 'the tree is my seat that once lent me shade'.

Hopkins continues in the environmentalist vein, comparing the damage we do to 'But a prick' which could destroy an eye. In this way, especially with the lines 'O if we but knew what we do / When we delve and hew', he seems way ahead of his time in hinting at what we now call ecology, or environmental interdependence.

Cowper in the earlier poem, however, goes on to reflect on the durability of man ('My fugitive years are all hasting away'), yet 'the perishing pleasures of man' are even shorter-lived.

Let's consider a pair of poems in more detail. Cats are always good for a poem.

Extract from *The Kitten at Play* by William Wordsworth (p. 136)

This extract has three sections: the opening couplet establishes the main theme of the poem, and the season; in the next ten lines, Wordsworth puts the kitten aside to concentrate on the movement of the falling leaves; and finally he expands on the theme of the kitten play-hunting the leaves.

These are not the 'usual' autumn leaves, being torn off the tree by the wind. The air is calm, and the morning is fair. The leaves are simply falling, with their movement governed only by gravity and their natural air-resistance: 'Eddying round and round they sink / Softly, slowly' as though fairies were surfing them towards the ground. The poem, like the leaves, has now reached the quick kitten who, in contrast to the lazy movements of the leaves, 'starts! / Crouches, stretches, paws, and darts'. The pace is briefly frantic as the kitten turns her attention from leaf to falling leaf, until the supply dwindles and stops. There's a hiatus as she looks up, willing another leaf to fall in her 'intentness of desire'.

When it does, this is no kitten sporting with the leaves, but a tigress hunting her prey; except . . . except, most kitten-like, she lets it go, just for the fun of catching it again. As they do. There's no 'fearful symmetry' in this tiger but, in Wordsworth's 'eye of fire', there **is** a hint of Blake's 'Tiger Tiger burning bright' (I wonder which was written first!).

This poem is all action: the writing maxim, 'show don't tell' (a subject which is explored more fully in *A Poetry Teacher's Toolkit* Book 4, Ch. 1).

In *On a Cat, Ageing* by Sir Alexander Gray (p. 137), the mouser may still have his 'night's adventures' but clearly he now prefers 'all the comforts / That Providence has sent'. The verbs are 'blinks', 'yawns' and 'purrs'; the adjectives are 'quiet' and 'restful'. This is one content cat! He long ago honed his hunting skills; he does his job and soaks up the rewards, seeing no end to this paradise with its constant supply of 'fish and milk and fish'. Nice touch that.

Does Gray need to use the word 'ageing' in his title? I don't think so. He doesn't need to **tell** us that the cat is getting old, because he **shows** us very clearly in the final stanza. It's still very passive: an unwelcome thought intruding on the cat's self-satisfaction. But the last two lines:

The times somehow are breeding
A nimbler race of mice.

have all the echoes of the human 'Fings ain't what they used to be', with the implication that he is starting to miss his kill. Only 'once or twice' mind you! This cat is not old yet, but he's certainly ageing.

THE LITERACY HOUR: YEARS 3 AND 4

National Literacy Strategy objectives: Years 3 and 4

Year 3
- To read aloud and recite poems, comparing different views of the same subject.
- To take account of the grammar and punctuation when reading aloud.
- To infer the meaning of unknown words from the context.

Year 4
- To compare and contrast poems on similar themes . . . discussing personal responses and preferences.
- To understand the significance of word order.
- To use word banks and dictionaries.

Chosen poems

The Phoenix by Robert Fisher (p. 129)
Roasting the Phoenix by Jane Clarke (p. 130)

Materials needed

Book of legends and myths containing account and illustration of a phoenix (not essential)
Enlarged copies of the chosen poems (see 'Preparation')
Activity sheets (see 'Preparation')
Flipchart or board
Marker pens
Activity sheets (see 'Preparation')
Pens, pencils, writing paper/books
Dictionaries and thesauruses
Anthologies containing poems dealing with the same theme or subject (of teacher's choice)
Stimulus cards (see 'Preparation')
White cards (postcard size) and a box to put them in

Preparation

Enlarge the chosen poems.

Make copies of the activity sheets for each child, according to achievement level (photocopiable sheets 4a, 4b, 4c on pp. 123–125).

Make two columns on the board, headed 'Similarities' and 'Differences'.

Make a set of cards each with a stimulus theme for poems. For example, 'Little sisters', 'Ghosts', 'Cabbage' or 'School assembly'.

With the whole class

- Ask the children whether they know what a phoenix is. Spend a few minutes talking about the story behind this mythical bird. If possible show them a picture from a book of myths and legends.
- Tell the children they're going to explore two poems about a phoenix and they should try to think how the poems are different.
- Share *The Phoenix* by Robert Fisher letting the children see the text as you read. When you have finished, ask them whether they enjoyed the poem. Why or why not? Is the poem close to the myth? How? Encourage the children to refer to the specific words or phrases that support their opinions.
- Does the poem have a verse pattern? (Four verses of six lines each.) What is the rhyme pattern of each verse? (AABCCB) Why does the poet use capital letters for 'BORN AGAIN'?
- Do the children think this poem is funny, interesting, sad, exciting, etc? List key words on the board for their impressions of the poem and leave them up.
- Tell them that now they're going to explore the second poem about a phoenix. Share *Roasting the Phoenix* by Jane Clarke letting the children follow the text as you read.
- When you have finished ask them whether they enjoyed the poem. Why or why not? Does the poem refer to the myth? How? Are there any words or phrases that the children are unsure of? For example, 'raging furnace' or 'funeral pyre'. Encourage them to work out the meanings from the context.
- Does the poem have a verse pattern? (Six verses of four lines each.) What is the rhyme pattern of each verse? (ABCB)
- Did the children find this poem funny? Can they say why or why not? Look at the key words on the board about *The Phoenix* and see whether any of them would be appropriate for *Roasting the Phoenix*.
- Help the children to compare the two poems. Some points you could explore are: *Roasting the Phoenix* is a narrative poem, but *The Phoenix* is not; *The Phoenix* is a poetic form of the myth, whereas *Roasting the Phoenix* is a story that relies on, but doesn't actually relate, the myth; *The Phoenix* is a 'straight' poem, but *Roasting the Phoenix* is humorous; both poems have a regular rhyme pattern; both poems have a recognisable, and mostly regular, verse pattern; both poems refer to people, even though the poem is about the bird ('Mum', 'Dad', 'I', 'you'); both poems assume a possibility that the mythical bird actually exists ('. . . look in the fire-light / and a phoenix may come to rest' and 'This year, we're having Phoenix / for our Christmas dinner . . .').

- As each point is discussed, agree whether it should go into the 'Similarities' or 'Differences' column on the board. Put key words into the agreed column and leave them up for the group session.
- Which poem do the children prefer? Why? Are there other mythical creatures that would make good subjects for a poem? For example, gorgons, unicorns or griffins. List them on the board. Tell the children they're going to do some more work on the poems in their groups.

Group and independent work (differentiated groups)

Group 1

Give an anthology to the group and ask them to find at least two poems on the same theme. Help them to read the poems and discuss how the theme is approached. Remind them to think of similarities and differences – they could look at the key words on the board for support. Nominate a scribe to make notes of the group's conclusions.

Group 2

Give the stimulus cards to the group. Let the children work in pairs and choose a card. They should then write a short poem based on the theme written on their card. Tell them that some of their poems will be used for comparisons during the plenary session. Remind them that their poems don't have to rhyme, and the pairs must work independently of each other.

Group 3

Give out the activity sheets 4a (for lower achievers), 4b (for average achievers) and 4c (for higher achievers) for the children to complete. Let them refer to the key words written on the board during the whole-class session to jog their memories.

Group 4

Give the group two or three anthologies, the white cards and the box. Ask the children to look through the anthologies for thematic ideas. They should make a 'Theme Bank': ask them to identify a subject or theme, write it as a heading on a card and then list the poems and the anthology. Use the bank later as a stimulus for writing poetry, as a reference for finding published theme poetry and as a working support for the children.

Plenary session (whole class)

- Ask some of the children who wrote poems on the same theme to read their work. Spend some time comparing the different approaches. Encourage the class to discover similarities and differences between the poems.
- What have the children learnt by exploring how different poets treat the same theme? During their group session, did they discover anything new about making comparisons? Do they enjoy work like this? Why or why not?

THE LITERACY HOUR: YEARS 5 AND 6

National Literacy Strategy objectives: Years 5 and 6

Year 5
- To analyse and compare poetic style . . . and themes of . . . poets.
- To understand the need for punctuation as an aid to the reader.
- To use dictionaries efficiently to explore . . . meanings.

Year 6
- To discuss how linked poems relate to one another by themes.
- To revise the conventions of standard English.
- To understand how words and expressions have changed over time.

Chosen poems

To the Cuckoo by William Wordsworth (p. 134)
The Cuckoo Comes in April, Anon (p. 133)

Materials needed

Picture of a cuckoo (not essential)
Enlarged copies of the chosen poems (see 'Preparation')
Flipchart or board
Marker pens
Activity sheets (see 'Preparation')
Pens, pencils, writing paper/books
Dictionaries and thesauruses
Copy of *To the Cuckoo* for each child in Group 1
Anthologies of poetry with themes

Preparation

Enlarge the chosen poems.
    Make copies of the activity sheets for each child, according to achievement level (photocopiable sheets 4aa, 4bb, 4cc on pp. 126–128).
    Divide an A4 sheet in half lengthways and head the columns 'Similarities' and 'Differences'. Make enough copies for Group 3.

With the whole class

- Before sharing the poems, spend a few minutes talking about the cuckoo. What do the children know about it? For example, that it lays one egg in another bird's nest; that it throws the host bird's eggs out of the nest to ensure the survival of its own egg; that it sings just once a year in springtime; that its song sounds like its name (i.e. onomatopoeic); that it is a dull grey-brown colour and that it is larger than most of our other common birds. If possible, show a picture of a cuckoo to the class.
- Share *To the Cuckoo* with the children. Make sure you read it with fluency, intonation and sense, to capture and retain the children's interest and attention. Can anyone tell you what William Wordsworth is trying to convey in his poem? Does he like cuckoos? How do we know? Encourage the children to refer to specific words and phrases to support their answers.
- Are there any words that the children don't understand? For example, 'blithe', 'visionary', 'beget' or 'faery place'. Help them to work out the meanings either through the context or using the dictionaries.
- What words or phrases tell us that this poem is 'old-fashioned'? For example, 'thee', 'Thy', Thrice' or 'Yet thou art'. Can anyone tell you what the modern equivalents of these are? Are we able to grasp the meaning of the poem despite the old-fashioned words?
- What does the poet think of when he hears the cuckoo for the first time each spring? (His childhood days) Did he enjoy those times? How do we know? ('That golden time') Does the poem have a verse pattern? Is it regular? What is the rhyme pattern?
- Now share *The Cuckoo Comes in April* – ask a volunteer to read it. What is this poem saying about the cuckoo? Are there any words or phrases that the children don't understand? Are we able to guess what the poet thinks about the cuckoo? Why or why not? Can we tell whether the poem is modern or older? Why or why not?
- Ask the children to compare the two poems, thinking about similarities and differences. For example, both have a rhyme pattern, both are about the cuckoo and both tell us when the cuckoo sings; *The Cuckoo Comes in April* is a straightforward statement of the cuckoo's spring cycle, but *To the Cuckoo* is an ode to the bird; *The Cuckoo Comes in April* is much shorter than *To the Cuckoo*; *To the Cuckoo* has archaic poetic language but *The Cuckoo Comes in April* has easy-to-follow, 'modern' language. Divide the board into halves, headed 'Similarities' and 'Differences'. Write in the appropriate column key words for each point the children make. Leave these up for the group session.
- Which poem do the children prefer? Why? Encourage them to express their opinions, making sure that 'negative' ones are listened to with respect by everyone.

Group and independent work (differentiated groups)

Group 1

Give each child a copy of *The Cuckoo Comes in April*. Ask the group to work together to learn the poem for a performance. They should make up some actions to go with their poem. Tell them they will have the chance to show the others their work at the plenary session.

Group 2

Give out copies of the activity sheets 4aa (for lower achievers), 4bb (for average achievers) and 4cc (for higher achievers) for the children to complete. They should use dictionaries and thesauruses for support.

Group 3

Give each child an A4 sheet divided into two columns (see 'Preparation'). Ask them to list the similarities and differences between *To the Cuckoo* and *The Cuckoo Comes in April*. Let them refer to the list written during the whole-class session for support.

Group 4

Give the group the poetry anthologies and ask the children to explore them. Ask them to choose one or two themes and at least two poems on the chosen themes. As a group, they should brainstorm the similarities and differences between their chosen poems and list these.

Plenary session (whole class)

- What have the children learnt by comparing two or more poems on the same theme? Do they enjoy doing this? Why or why not?
- Which is their favourite cuckoo poem? Encourage them to give reasons for their answers.
- Ask the group who practised a performance of *The Cuckoo Comes in April* to show the class their work. Let them teach the actions to the class and then have a class recital.

SHEET 4a

Name _____

Read *The Phoenix* by Robert Fisher and *Roasting the Phoenix* by Jane Clarke.

Write 'True' or 'False' next to each of these sentences:

Roasting the Phoenix is a narrative poem. _____

The Phoenix has a regular verse pattern. _____

The Phoenix is a humorous poem. _____

Roasting the Phoenix has a regular rhyme pattern. _____

Write one more similarity and one more difference between *Roasting the Phoenix* and *The Phoenix*:

Similarity _____

Difference _____

Draw a phoenix here:

SHEET 4b

Name _____

Read *The Phoenix* by Robert Fisher and *Roasting the Phoenix* by Jane Clarke.

Write 'True' or 'False' next to each of these sentences:

The Phoenix is a narrative poem. _____

Roasting the Phoenix has a regular verse pattern. _____

The Phoenix is a poem about the myth. _____

Roasting the Phoenix is not a humorous poem. _____

The Phoenix has a regular rhyme pattern. _____

Roasting the Phoenix is a poem about the myth. _____

Write two more similarities and differences between *Roasting the Phoenix* and *The Phoenix*:

Similarity _____

Difference _____

Similarity _____

Difference _____

Draw a phoenix here:

SHEET 4c

Name _____

Read *The Phoenix* by Robert Fisher and *Roasting the Phoenix* by Jane Clarke.

Write 'True' or 'False' next to each of these sentences:

Roasting the Phoenix has a regular rhyme pattern. _____

The Phoenix is not a poem about the myth. _____

Roasting the Phoenix has a regular verse pattern. _____

The Phoenix is not a narrative poem. _____

Roasting the Phoenix is a humorous poem. _____

The Phoenix is a poem about the myth. _____

Roasting the Phoenix has a regular verse pattern. _____

The Phoenix does not have a regular verse pattern. _____

Write two more similarities and differences between *Roasting the Phoenix* and *The Phoenix*:

Similarity _____

Difference _____

Similarity _____

Difference _____

Draw a phoenix here:

© Collette Drifte and Mike Jubb (2002) *A Poetry Teacher's Toolkit*, Book 3. London: David Fulton Publishers.

SHEET 4aa

Name _____

Read this poem:

The Cuckoo Comes in April

The cuckoo comes in April,
He sings his song in May;
In the middle of June
He changes his tune,
And then he flies away.

Now complete this poem about a cuckoo. You could use the words at the bottom, or make up your own. Remember that your poem doesn't have to rhyme.

The Cuckoo

When it's April, the cuckoo _____

When it's May, she _____

In another bird's nest she _____

And when it's June she _____

     leaves   flies   egg   sings   lays   comes

Write a difference and a similarity between *The Cuckoo Comes in April* and your poem.

Similarity _____

Difference _____

© Collette Drifte and Mike Jubb (2002) *A Poetry Teacher's Toolkit*, Book 3. London: David Fulton Publishers.

SHEET 4bb

Name _____

Read this poem:

The Cuckoo Comes in April

The cuckoo comes in April,
He sings his song in May;
In the middle of June
He changes his tune,
And then he flies away.

Now complete this poem about a cuckoo. You could use the words at the bottom, or make up your own. Remember that your poem doesn't have to rhyme.

The Cuckoo

In April, the cuckoo _____
She _____ in May,
She _____ other birds' eggs
And _____ in June.

song   goes   flies   arrives   egg   sings   hides   comes

Write two differences and two similarities between *The Cuckoo Comes in April* and your poem.

Similarity _____

Difference _____

Similarity _____

Difference _____

SHEET 4cc

Name _____

Read this poem:

The Cuckoo Comes in April

The cuckoo comes in April,
He sings his song in May;
In the middle of June
He changes his tune,
And then he flies away.

Now write a poem about a cuckoo. Remember that your poem doesn't have to rhyme.

The Cuckoo

_____

_____

_____

_____

Write three differences and three similarities between *The Cuckoo Comes in April* and your poem.

Similarity _____

Difference _____

Similarity _____

Difference _____

Similarity _____

Difference _____

The Phoenix

Robert Fisher

The phoenix in its flight
through the forests of the night
is seeking a place to rest.
With its rainbow-coloured wings
and its purple rings
it is searching for a nest.

This bird is rare
it feeds on air
and flies by like a dream.
When you're alone at night
it will give you a fright
when you hear its eerie scream.

The phoenix lives in fire
and its one desire
is to enter the flickering flame.
It flutters and burns
and to ash it turns
and then it is BORN AGAIN!

Of all the breeds of bird
of which you've ever heard
the phoenix is the best.
When you get home tonight
look in the fire-light
and a phoenix may come to rest.

Roasting the Phoenix

Jane Clarke

This year, we're having Phoenix
for our Christmas dinner,
and if Mum doesn't burn it,
it's sure to be a winner.

Oh no! The oven's smoking,
our dinner's catching fire.
It's a raging furnace,
a Phoenix funeral pyre.

Mum puts on the oven gloves,
then she lets out a roar –
'That Phoenix has grown feathers,
it's fluttering at the door!

Help! Somebody let it out!
This is a job for Dad!
I'm sorry that I stuffed it,
it's looking really mad!'

So Dad opens the oven
and the bird soars off in flight!
Mum has to have a sherry,
She's had a fearful fright.

It rose up from the ashes,
so dinner's off, I fear,
I wish we'd had a turkey,
like every other year!

Binsey Poplars, felled 1879

Gerard Manley Hopkins

My aspens dear, whose airy cages quelled,
Quelled or quenched in leaves the leaping sun,
All felled, felled, are all felled;
   Of a fresh and following folded rank
      Not one spared, not one
      That dandled a sandalled
     Shadow that swam or sank
On meadow and river and wind-wandering
   weed-winding bank.

O if we but knew what we do
      When we delve and hew –
Hack and rack the growing green!
      Since country is so tender
To touch, her being so slender,
That, like this sleek and seeing ball
But a prick will make no eye at all,
Where we, even where we mean
      To mend her we end her,
     When we hew or delve:
After-comers cannot guess the beauty been.
   Ten or twelve, only ten or twelve
     Strokes of havoc únselve
      The sweet especial scene,
     Rural scene, a rural scene,
     Sweet especial rural scene.

The Poplar Field

William Cowper

The poplars are felled; farewell to the shade
And the whispering sound of the cool colonnade;
The winds play no longer and sing in the leaves,
Nor Ouse on his bosom their image receives.

Twelve years have elapsed since I first took a view
Of my favourite field and the bank where they grew:
And now in the grass behold they are laid,
And the tree is my seat that once lent me shade.

The blackbird has fled to another retreat,
Where hazels afford him a screen from the heat;
And the scene where his melody charmed me before
Resounds with his sweet-flowing ditty no more.

My fugitive years are all hasting away,
And I must ere long lie as lowly as they,
With a turf on my breast and a stone at my head,
Ere another such grove shall arise in its stead.

'Tis a sight to engage me, if anything can,
To muse on the perishing pleasures of man;
Though his life be a dream, his enjoyments, I see,
Have a being less durable even than he.

The Cuckoo Comes in April

Anon.

The cuckoo comes in April,
He sings his song in May;
In the middle of June
He changes his tune,
And then he flies away.

The Cuckoo

Anon.

In April
Come he will,
In flow'ry May
He sings all day,
In leafy June
He changes his tune,
In bright July
He's ready to fly,
In August
Go he must.

To the Cuckoo

William Wordsworth

O blithe new-comer! I have heard,
I hear thee, and rejoice:
O Cuckoo! shall I call thee bird
Or but a wandering voice?

While I am lying on the grass,
Thy two-fold shout I hear;
From hill to hill it seems to pass,
At once far off, and near.

Though babbling only to the vale
Of sunshine and of flowers,
Thou bringest unto me a tale
Of visionary hours.

Thrice, welcome, darling of the Spring!
Even yet thou art to me
No bird, but an invisible thing,
A voice, a mystery.

The same whom in my schoolboy days
I listened to; that cry
Which made me look a thousand ways
In bush, and tree, and sky.

To seek thee did I often rove
Through woods and on the green;
And thou wert still a hope, a love;
Still longed for, never seen.

To the Cuckoo **(continued)**

And I can listen to thee yet;
Can lie upon the plain
And listen, till I do beget
That golden time again.

O blessed bird! the earth we pace
Again appears to be
An unsubstantial, faery place;
That is fit home for Thee!

Extract from *The Kitten at Play*

William Wordsworth

See the kitten on the wall,
Sporting with the leaves that fall,
Withered leaves – one, two and three –
From the lofty elder tree!
Through the calm and frosty air
Of this morning bright and fair,
Eddying round and round they sink
Softly, slowly: one might think
From the motions that are made,
Every little leaf conveyed
Sylph or fairy, hither tending –
To this lower world descending,
Each invisible and mute,
In his wavering parachute.
– But the kitten, how she starts!
Crouches, stretches, paws, and darts:
First at one, and then its fellow,
Just as light and just as yellow;
There are many now – now one –
Now they stop; and there are none.
What intentness of desire
In her up-turned eye of fire!
With a tiger-leap half way,
Now she meets the coming prey.
Lets it go at last, and then
Has it in her power again.

On a Cat, Ageing

Sir Alexander Gray

He blinks upon the hearth-rug
  And yawns in deep content,
Accepting all the comforts
  That Providence has sent.

Louder he purrs, and louder,
  In one glad hymn of praise
For all the night's adventures,
  For quiet, restful days.

Life will go on for ever,
  With all that a cat can wish;
Warmth and the glad procession
  Of fish and milk and fish.

Only – the thought disturbs him –
  He's noticed once or twice,
That times somehow are breeding
  A nimbler race of mice.

The Moon

Katy Ware (age 10)

(Redlands Primary School, Fareham – with a little help from Mummy, Helen)

Man on the moon, first trip for me.
Off on a mission, to see what I can see.
Off on an adventure, let's search this galaxy.
Neil Armstrong's my name, as reported on T.V.

Up in the Sky

Rachael Oliver (age 10)

(Redlands Primary School, Fareham)

Up in
    the sky
        is the moon
with the star dust
        flowing around
it with all the little
    Aliens doing the moon walk.

The Moon

Dan Fisher (age 10)

(Redlands Primary School, Fareham – with a little help from Mum and Dad)

Against my thumb you look so small,
You remind me of a snooker ball.
As I lie and stare at you,
I use my finger as a cue.

Like a fried egg in the sky,
I wonder how you got so high.
As I sit and stare at you,
I want to stick my fork in you.

Perhaps one day there will be a bus,
Flying round the universe,
I'm sure you're just as curious,
I wonder what you think of us . . . ?

The Bewitching Hour

Elizabeth Bailey (age 10)

(Redlands Primary School, Fareham)

The silvery moon glows
in the midnight sky,
casting ghostly shadows across the land, while
children sleep soundly in their beds.

The bewitching hour draws near
for all the beasts and creatures of
the night.

Further Reading

This is not meant to be a definitive list of poetry books for children, just a few that we particularly like (apologies for all the great collections that we've left out).

Reference

Roget's Thesaurus
The Penguin Rhyming Dictionary
The Oxford Spelling Dictionary

Collections by individual poets

Gerard Benson, *The Magnificent Callisto* (Blackie 1992)
Charles Causley, *Collected Poems for Children* (Macmillan UK 1996)
Eleanor Farjeon, *Blackbird Has Spoken* (Macmillan UK 1999)
John Foster, *Word Wizard* (Oxford University Press 2001)
Lindsay MacRae, *How to Avoid Kissing Your Parents in Public* (Puffin 2000)
Colin McNaughton, *There's an Awful Lot of Weirdos in our Neighbourhood* (Walker Books 2000)
Gareth Owen, *Collected Poems for Children* (Macmillan UK 2000)
Brian Patten, *Juggling with Gerbils* (Puffin 2000)
Robert Louis Stevenson, *A Child's Garden of Verses* (various editions available)
J. R. R. Tolkien, *The Adventures of Tom Bombadil* (George Allen and Unwin 1961)

Anthologies

John Agard and Grace Nichols (eds) *A Caribbean Dozen* (Walker Books 1994)
John Agard, Wendy Cope, Roger McGough, Adrian Mitchell, Brian Patten and Colin McNaughton, *Another Day on Your Foot and I Would Have Died* (Macmillan Children's Books 1996)
Jill Bennett and Mary Rees, *Spooky Poems* (Heinemann 1989)
Jill Bennett and Nick Sharratt, *Playtime Poems* (Oxford University Press 1995)
John Foster, *A First Poetry Book* (Oxford University Press 1979)
John Foster, *Another First Poetry Book* (Oxford University Press 1987)
John Foster, *Another Second Poetry Book* (Oxford University Press 1988)
John Foster, *Let's Celebrate Festival Poems* (Oxford University Press 1989)

John Foster, *A Blue Poetry Paintbox* (Oxford University Press 1994)

John Foster, *A Green Poetry Paintbox* (Oxford University Press 1994)

John Foster, *Action Rhymes* (Oxford University Press 1996)

John Foster, *Crack Another Yolk and other wordplay poems* (Oxford University Press 1996)

John Foster, *First Verses* (Oxford University Press 1996)

John Foster, *Food Rhymes* (Oxford University Press 1998)

John Foster, *More First Verses* (Oxford University Press 1998)

Sophie Hannah, *The Box Room* (Orchard Books 2001) (recommended pantoum called *The Swimming Pool*)

Brian Moses, *Performance Poems* (Southgate 1996)

Brian Patten (ed.) *The Puffin Book of Utterly Brilliant Poetry* (Puffin Books 2001)

Michael Rosen, *A Spider Bought a Bicycle and other poems for young children* (Kingfisher Books 1992)

Will Self, *Junk Mail* (Penguin 1996)

Kaye Umansky, *Nonsense Counting Rhymes* (Oxford University Press 1999)

Shape poetry

Paul Cookson, *The Works* (Macmillan 2001)

Gina Douthwaite, *Picture a Poem* (Hutchinson 1994)

Gina Douthwaite, *What Shapes an Ape?* (Hutchinson 2001)

John Foster, *Crack Another Yolk* (Oxford University Press 1996)

Magazine

Literacy and Learning, published by the Questions Publishing Company Ltd

Glossary

Acrostic
A poetic form which is organised by the initial letters of a key word, either at the beginning of lines, or with lines arranged around them.

Whistling wildly   Blowing
In a   rain
Northern   round
Direction   and round

Adagio
A slow tempo.

Alliteration
A phrase in which adjacent or closely connected words begin with the same phoneme: one wet Wellington; free phone; several silent, slithering snakes.

Alphabets
Poems based on alphabetical order.

Ambigram
This is one name given to words that can be read in more than one way, or from more than one vantage point, either as themselves such as 'NOON' and 'suns' (upside down), or as a different word ('PAT'/'TAP'). Obviously, this ties in well with symmetry, and upper case gives different results from lower.

Anagram
A word or phrase formed by rearranging the letters of another word or phrase.

Analysis
An examination of the elements within a poem.

Anthology
A published collection of poems by several or many poets.

Anthropomorphism
Attributing human qualities to animals. See also **Personification**.

Antonym
A word with a meaning opposite to another: hot/cold, light/dark, light/heavy.
A word may have more than one word as an antonym: cold – hot/warm; big – small/tiny/little/titchy. See **Thesaurus**.

Appreciation
Added enjoyment of poetry through some knowledge of its elements. See **Analysis**.

Archaic language
No longer in ordinary use, though possibly retained for special purposes. The National Literacy Strategy requires that children learn 'to identify clues which suggest poems are older'.

Assonance
The rhyming of vowel sounds (but not consonants) in nearby words: such as in 'time' and 'light'. There is some overlap with near-rhymes here, because assonance is also the use of identical consonants with different vowels: such as in
chilled/called/fold/mild/failed/hurled.

Beat
Main accent or rhythmic unit in music or verse.

Brainstorming
A joint discussion about a particular subject in order to pool knowledge, and to generate new ideas.

Caesura
A pause in a line of poetry (either at the end of the line, or mid-line), indicated by punctuation, a line break, or the natural flow of the language.

Calligram
A poem, or graphic, in which the calligraphy, the formation of the letters or the font selected, represents an aspect of the poem's subject: a poem about fear might be written in shaky letters to represent trembling; the word BRICKS could be printed in a brick-type font. See **Concrete poem** and **Shape poetry**.

Cinquain
A poem with a standard syllable pattern: 5 lines and a total of 22 syllables in the sequence: 2–4–6–8–2.

Cliché
An overused phrase or opinion: over the moon; flogging a dead horse; as sure as eggs is eggs.

Compound words
A word made up of two or more other words. There are three forms of compound word:
 closed form: football, headrest, broomstick
 hyphenated form: son-in-law, over-the-counter, six-year-old
 open form: post office, frying pan, full moon

Concrete poem
A poem in which the layout of the words represents some aspect of the subject. In some cases, these poems are presented as sculptures. Concrete poems blur the distinction between visual and linguistic art. See also **Calligram** and **Shape poetry**.

Crescendo
A passage gradually increasing in loudness or intensity; progress towards a climax.

Dactyl
A metrical foot consisting of one long (or stressed) syllable followed by two short (or unstressed) syllables (˘ ˉ ˉ): **butt**er-fly, **round**about, **bick**ering.

Diminuendo
A passage gradually decreasing in loudness or intensity.

Drafting/redrafting
The writing of initial and subsequent versions of a text, incorporating changes or revisions before the final version.

Dynamics
In poetry, as in music, a good performance requires variations in pace, pitch and volume. See also **Adagio**; **Caesura**; **Crescendo**; **Diminuendo**; **Pitch**; **Presto**; **Tempo**; **Timbre**.

Emphasis
A stress on a particular letter, phoneme, syllable or word.

Enjambment
In poetry, the continuation of a sentence without pause beyond the end of a line.

Exact rhyme
See **Rhyme**.

Expression
Using intonation to convey the meaning of a text. See also **Performance**.

Found verse
A piece of prose, from a source such as a newspaper, which is edited and presented as a poem.

Free verse
Poetry which is not constrained by patterns of rhyme or rhythm.

Full rhyme
See **Rhyme**.

Gunsaku
A group of haiku or tanka on a single subject which illuminates the subject from various

points of view, but can be read independently; e.g. a group of children could tackle the subject of 'Winter' by sharing out combinations of the following aspects: weather, animal hibernation, migration, difficulties for birds and animals, deciduous trees, conifers, a festival, colour, day length, etc.

Haiku

A Japanese form of poetry, widely thought in the West to be three lines of 5–7–5 syllables respectively. In truth, the form is much more flexible than that. It has always evolved, and is still evolving.

Half-rhymes

Multi-syllabic words in which the final syllable rhymes, e.g. camping/jumping. One of the examples of a half-rhyme given in the glossary of the National Literacy Strategy is 'polish/relish'. The other example given ('pun/man') is, in fact, classed as *near-rhyme*. See also **Rhyme**.

Hidden words

A type of wordplay in which one word is 'hidden' in the conjunction of two others. For example,

where do you hide a house?

round people *who use*d to live in a field

Homophones

Words that sound the same but have different meanings, and often different spellings.

Iamb (or Iambus)/Iambic

A metrical foot consisting of one short (or unstressed) syllable followed by one long (or stressed) syllable (⁻ �‿): I **wan**dered **lonely as** a **cloud** that **floats** on **high** o'er **vales** and **hills.**

INSET

In-service education and training. Further training or professional development for teachers or other educational practitioners.

Internal rhyme

The placement of rhyming words within a line of poetry, rather than at the end. The National Literacy Strategy example is:

'Th**ough** the threat of sn**ow** was gr**ow**ing sl**ow**ly'; in fact, 'gr**ow**ing sl**ow**ly' is *assonance*.

Intonation

The modulation of the voice during speech or reading.

Kenning

A compound expression used in Old English and Norse poetry, which names something without using its name, e.g. *mouse catcher = cat*. A kenning is, therefore, not a poem in itself, but a poem can be a list of kennings about one subject.

Kick-offs

Within this series, a *kick-off* is a strategy that will get children writing immediately, without 'thinking' too much.

Layout

The physical arrangement of words on the page.

Limerick

A five-line verse, usually comic, with the rhyme scheme AABBA, and the following stress pattern.

A **dark**-haired young **Prin**cess was **fond**
Of **kiss**ing a **frog** in the **pond.**
But it **made** the frog **wince**
Cos he **wasn't** a **prince,**
And be**sides** that, he **want**ed a **blonde.**
[M.J.]

Line break

The point at which a poet chooses to end a line. This is particularly relevant to non-metric poetry in which line breaks are used as a form of punctuation.

Metaphor

Where the writer writes about something as if it were really something else. A metaphor can take several forms: his voice was thunder; his thunderous voice; his voice of thunder, the thunder of his voice. See also **Personification** and **Simile**.

Meter

Lines of poetry with a specified number of measures (or feet), e.g. a pentameter has five measures. There are various types of metrical foot. See **Dactyl**, **Iamb**, and **Trochee**.

Monosyllabic
Words or sounds consisting of only one syllable (and they have to invent a five-syllable word to describe it!).

Narrative poem
A poem that tells a story.

National Literacy Strategy
The official literacy curriculum taught in state schools in England and Wales.

Near-rhymes
Ones that you can get away with if you're not a slave to exact rhyme, e.g. can/men; stricken/picking. It's subjective; what the poet is happy with, because meaning is more important. See **Half-rhymes** and **Rhyme**.

Nonsense poems
A poem 'not of this world', but which makes perfect sense within its own parameters. There is a grey area between 'nonsense' and 'fantasy'.

Objectives
The educational targets or goals of the National Literacy Strategy.

Onji
Japanese sound units similar to, but different from, syllables.

Onomatopoeia
Words that echo sounds associated with their meaning: clang, hiss, crash, cuckoo.

Palindrome
A word or phrase that is the same when read left–right or right–left: kayak; Hannah; was it a cat I saw. Palindromes also exist where the word order is reversed, e.g. You and Mary only saw sweet Sally Little, and little Sally Sweet saw only Mary and you.

Pantoum/Pantun
A form of poetry originating in Malaysia in which the second line of each verse becomes the first line of the following verse, sometimes with a slight variation. There may also be a link between the final and the first verses making the poem 'circular'.

Patterns
Regular formats found within poetry. They can be patterns of rhyme, rhythm, verse or line, for example.

Pentameter
A line of poetry consisting of five metrical feet.

Performance
The reciting of a poem using expression, intonation, pitch, volume, facial gestures and actions to convey the meaning, i.e. not simply reading the text.

Personification
A form of *metaphor* in which language relating to human action, motivation and emotion is used to refer to non-human agents or objects or abstract concepts, e.g. The chair obviously resented this demand on its strength; His jealousy took charge of him.

Pitch
The degrees of highness or lowness of the tone of voice during speech.

Polysyllabic
Words or sounds of more than one syllable.

Portmanteau words
New words that are blended from two or more existing words: brunch = breakfast + lunch; to crawble = to crawl under the table.

Prefix
A morpheme that can be added to the beginning of a word to change its meaning: in/edible, un/controllable, dis/agreeable.

Presto
Quick tempo.

Prose
Written language which does not follow poetic or dramatic forms.

Pun
A play on words, e.g. the maths teacher had divided loyalties; use of words with similar sounds, but different meaning, to 'humorous' effect, e.g. 'I can't bare it,' said Teddy.

Quatrain
A verse of four lines, usually with alternate rhymes.

Recite
To repeat aloud a poem from memory, particularly as a *performance*.

Redrafting
See **Drafting/redrafting**.

Redundancies
Words or phrases that can be removed from a text without affecting its essential meaning.

Reflected alliteration
Collette Drifte's term for alliteration that is transposed or 'reflected', e.g. . . . *chance of shade / cushion in the chair* (from *Home* by Rupert Brooke).

Rensaku
A longer work composed of individual haiku or tanka which function as stanzas of the whole, and are not independent.

Rhyme, Exact rhyme and Full rhyme
Words containing the same rime in their final syllable, or syllables, are said to rhyme. Single-syllable rhymes, e.g. moon/spoon, are referred to as male rhymes; where more than one syllable rhymes, e.g. dressing/messing, these are said to be female rhymes. See **Half-rhymes** and **Near-rhymes**.

Rhyming couplet
Two successive lines which rhyme at the ends.

Rhyming dictionary
A book of wordlists arranged according to rhyme. There's more than one on the market, but *The Penguin Rhyming Dictionary* (ISBN 0-14-051136-9) is very user friendly and is highly recommended.

Rhyming slang
An idiomatic form of speech where the spoken phrase rhymes with its (usually unspoken) meaning. For example, 'apples and pears' meaning 'stairs'. The two best known forms of rhyming slang are Cockney and Australian.

Rhythm
A pattern formed by a measured flow of words determined by long and short and/or accented and unaccented syllables.

Shape poetry
A generic term, covering both *calligrams* and *concrete poems*; a poem in which layout of the words reflects an aspect of the subject.

Show don't tell
A writer's 'trick of the trade'. It is generally stronger writing to say, for example, 'He banged his fist on the table' (showing the emotion) than 'He was angry' (merely telling).

Simile
A figure of speech involving the comparison of one thing with another thing of a different kind, as an illustration or ornament. Similes usually, but not necessarily, contain the word 'like' or 'as': 'He felt like a duck in the desert'; 'As quiet as a cloud'. See also **Metaphor** and **Personification**.

Spoonerism
Transposition of the initial letters of two words, giving an alternate phrase. For example, 'a darling snog'.

Stanza
A 'verse' or set of lines in poetry, the pattern of which is often repeated throughout the poem. However, stanzas can be of different lengths within the same poem.

Stress
An accent or emphasis on a word or syllable.

Structure
The format or layout of a text.

Suffix
A morpheme that is added to the end of a word. For example, 'scope' in 'telescope' and 'microscope'.

Syllable
A phonetic unit usually consisting of one vowel sound with a consonant before and after.

Synonyms
Words that have the same, or very similar, meaning: little/small. English is so rich in synonyms that overuse of any word is easily avoided. See **Thesaurus**.

Tanka
Meaning 'short poem'. A Japanese poem that has a **typical** form of 5–7–5–7–7 *syllables* (Japanese *onji*). Tanka has a history of about 13 centuries, as opposed to about three centuries for *haiku*, so is **not** based on the haiku as stated in the National Literacy Strategy document.

Tautology
Use of an extra word in a phrase or sentence which unnecessarily repeats an idea: the **annual** event is staged **yearly**; a **sudden surge** of water ('sudden' being part of the meaning of 'surge'). See also **Redundancies**.

Template
A solid outline representing an object or shape, used to draw around.

Tempo
The speed at which a piece of poetry is *recited*. The tempo can be varied within a poem to give a more interesting *performance*.

Tetrameter
A line of poetry consisting of four metrical feet.

Thesaurus
A reference text which groups words and phrases by meaning and association.

Timbre
The distinctive character or tone of a voice used while *reciting*.

Tongue-twisters
A sequence of words which is difficult to pronounce correctly and/or quickly.

Trochee/trochaic
In poetry, a metrical foot consisting of a long followed by a short syllable, or an accented followed by an unaccented syllable, e.g. **Nev**er **on** a **Sun**day, **dar**ling.

Word morphing
A phrase coined to describe the transformation of one word into another by changing one letter, e.g. CAT → CAN. This can be expanded into strings, with three-letter words being easiest: CAT → CAN → MAN → MEN; FACE → FACT → PACT → PART → PORT; TWITS → TWINS → TWINE → SWINE → SHINE → SHONE.

Wordplay
A generic term which includes: *puns, word morphing, anagrams, calligrams, palindromes, hidden words.*

Index